MW00905272

On wings unfolded

On wings unfolded

A journey towards the light

BEVERLEY LITCHFIELD

Angus&Robertson
An imprint of HarperCollins*Publishers*

Angus & Robertson
An imprint of HarperCollins*Publishers*, (Australia)

First published in Australia in 1996
by HarperCollins*Publishers* Pty Limited
ACN 009 913 517
A member of the HarperCollins*Publishers* (Australia) Pty Limited Group

Copyright © Beverley Litchfield 1996

This book is copyright.
Apart from any fair dealing for the purposes of private study,
research, criticism or review, as permitted under the Copyright Act,
no part may be reproduced by any process without written
permission. Inquiries should be addressed to the publishers.

HarperCollins*Publishers*
25 Ryde Road, Pymble, Sydney NSW 2073, Australia
31 View Road, Glenfield, Auckland 10, New Zealand
77–85 Fulham Palace Road, London W6 8JB, United Kingdom
Hazelton Lanes, 55 Avenue Road, Suite 2900, Toronto, Ontario, M5R 3L2
and 1995 Markham Road, Scarborough, Ontario M1B 5M8, Canada
10 East 53rd Street, New York NY 10032, USA

The National Library of Australia Cataloguing-in-Publication data:

Litchfield, Beverley.
   On wings unfolded : a journey towards the light.

   ISBN 0 207 18982 X .

   1. Angels. 2. Future life. 3. Mental healing. 4. Healing –
   Religious aspects. 5. Near-death experiences – Religious
   aspects. I. Title.

291.215

Designed by Rosemarie Franzoni
Cover design by Rosemarie Franzoni
Cover illustration by Michelle Ryan
Author photo (back cover) by John Adey
Typeset in Australia by Emtype Desktop Publishing
Printed in Australia by Griffin Paperbacks

9 8 7 6 5 4 3 2 1
99 98 97 96

For He shall give His angels charge over thee,
to keep thee in all thy ways.
They shall bear thee up in their hands,
lest thou dash thy foot against a stone.

Psalm 91:11–12

$\mathcal{F}$oreword

We often bounce, cruise, lurch or flop through life, rarely looking inwards unless something happens to stop us in our tracks, usually something frightening. Most of us plough on, putting aside as too hard or unnecessary the notion of devoting as much energy to reflecting on our own lives as we give to reflecting on the lives of others. Indeed, from infancy many of us are taught to look to others for signals that tell us how we appear to them and whether we measure up in their eyes. When carried to extremes, this sort of behaviour can be quite literally soul-destroying.

The work I did with Beverley Litchfield changed the way I lived my life. She helped me find peace, calmness and joy – things that were available to me and exclusively mine if only I could train myself to see things differently. She gave me the opportunity to redefine my construct of reality so that I could sustain and support myself, instead of constantly criticising myself and feeling miserable.

The love that Beverley poured on me, over me and around me was wonderful and very powerful. She made me realise how few of us give love to ourselves and to each other and how fulfilling and rewarding the experience and knowledge of unconditional love can be. Beverley and her professional partner, John, who I also saw on a number of occasions, made me feel completely safe and totally protected and, more importantly, taught me how to take that feeling out the door and into my everyday life.

When we look back on a person's life, it is the essence of the person that emerges. The characteristics that determined their choices in life, their degrees of 'lightness' and 'darkness', their strengths and weaknesses, their attitudes and actions, the spirit that governed their responses to everything that life threw at them and the path they trod on their journey, tell us more about the person than any list of dates and places.

The essence of Beverley Litchfield emerges in *On wings unfolded*. The loving, vulnerable, kind, gentle, strong and determined individual that is Beverley shines through, and the clarity and purity of her message and of her love are a true inspiration.

I don't know how Beverley does what she does, but I'm very glad she does it and I'm extremely grateful to her and to John for their help. The story of Beverley's life journey and of her growth as a healer is fascinating, and certainly challenges the tired old notion that there is such a thing as coincidence.

Thank you for having the courage to share your story, Beverley.

Noni Hazlehurst

Contents

$\mathcal{P}$reface

I have worked as a psychic healer, clairvoyant and 'spiritual' counsellor for the past ten years. During that time, I have seen many thousands of people from all walks of life and have tried to the best of my ability to help them to understand themselves and the universe in a way that makes sense to me. I don't pretend that the philosophy that works for me will necessarily be right for you, the reader. I only wish to share with you what understanding I have. You must draw your own conclusions!

During the past fifteen years, I have shared my basic understandings of life with people I call my 'clients'. These are people who have visited me at my home and with whom, on average, I would spend one hour per session. During that time, I would 'look into' them to see who they are, where they have come from, and where they are going.

This, of course, sounds quite ridiculous to the logical mind and if you have never encountered a psychic you are probably thinking 'What rubbish!' I would have thought so too, if it had not been for my experience at these sessions, where over and over again I found myself 'picking up' knowledge and truth about complete strangers. Many of these strangers returned to see me time and time again and I am still psychically helping and advising many people whom I first met when I began to work in this fascinating field.

I decided to write this book because I want more people to have access to the ideas that I believe help to make sense out of confusion. The book is divided into four sections.

Part 1 is the story of my life and the important events and people in my psychic and spiritual development. This is important because it provides you with a background to my life and the experiences that led me to become a psychic counsellor and healer.

Part 2 is a statement about the philosophical assumptions about ourselves as human beings and why we have come to this earthly plane. It is these assumptions that guide and underpin my work.

Part 3 is material that has been given to me by a spiritual guide named Anna Maree. This is channelled information, dealing with important aspects of our life, aspects such as love, peace and wisdom.

Part 4, the final section of the book, is where many of the ideas of the first three sections come together in a series of case studies of readings for some of my clients. They illustrate my gift of being able to 'tune in' to the future and to sources of knowledge that lie outside of our bodies and minds.

We are all journeying through life. The journey is often confusing and we need to make order out of chaos in our minds. It can also be a very lonely experience. If this book helps you on your journey, then it has achieved its purpose.

Journey onwards in peace and understanding!

Acknowledgements

In preparing for this book and in actually writing the manuscript, I have been most grateful to the following people – all of whom I love dearly and without whose guidance and support this book would not have been written.

Firstly, to John, my friend, whose enthusiasm and love have been inspiring to me, and to Laurie, whose power-house of energy and love helped to light my way. I owe you both so much!

My eternal gratitude to my children Mark and Jayn, and to my ex-husband Michael, who put up with me throughout my trials and tribulations.

My sincere thanks to my mentors and to all of my clients, without whom my gift would not have been put to use.

A special thanks to David and Pauline, who spent time and energy in checking the manuscript, and who have helped to reinforce my belief in the Great Unknown.

A very special thanks to my dear friend Andrew, who believed in me and who encouraged me to keep going.

And last but not least, my deep appreciation for the loving guidance, support and understanding given by my husband Bruce, who inspired me to write this book.

I hope you enjoy my story!

Part one

The story of my psychic development

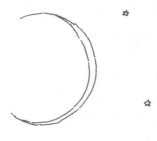

The early years

I want to tell you from the outset that I am a very ordinary human being. There is nothing outstanding about me, except perhaps my ability to 'know' things about other human beings.

But it wasn't always so.

I spent the first thirty-five years of my life as a very 'unknowing' person. I grew up in a working-class suburb of Sydney, Australia, with the most wonderful family any girl could have. My parents were hard-working and extremely loving human beings, especially to their family of three daughters. I am the middle daughter and sit somewhere in personality between my elder, more outgoing sister, Robyn, and my younger and very clever sister, Sue. I love them dearly and feel that they have all contributed to my genuine caring and compassion for human beings. Without such a warm, close-knit family, I believe I could not have developed my psychic gifts.

At the age of eighteen, I married and gave birth – still at the age of eighteen – to my son, Mark. At the time I was studying at teachers' college, and after Mark's birth I continued both to study for my teacher's certificate and to take care of my beautiful son. His father is an emotionally strong man and I believe his strength helped to give me the discipline I needed in order to achieve what life demanded of me.

Life was full. I studied hard, passed my examinations, and became a primary school teacher when Mark was one year old. I then found myself pregnant for a second time. This time I felt uneasy about the developing foetus but the doctors assured me that all was well.

I gave birth to a gorgeous little girl named Katherine Louise on 1 September – the first day of spring. What joy – a beautiful daughter. But my fears turned into reality. The nursing sister at the hospital informed me that my dear little girl had something wrong with her back. She wouldn't elaborate on this because the doctor who was to deliver the baby hadn't bothered to attend the confinement. The sister felt obliged to keep the final news about my baby for the doctor to tell me. I was feeling both elated and alarmed.

Finally, the doctor arrived and with him came the ambulance officers. I was not allowed to hold my baby girl in my arms and all I could do was watch as she was taken by the ambulance officer and placed in a humidicrib. I noticed that she had thick black hair and that she was tiny.

The doctor spoke to me in a very matter-of-fact voice. He told me that my daughter had been born with a condition called spina bifida which meant that there was a hole at the base of her spine. I was so thrilled to have a daughter that I assured him that this was only a minor problem to me and that (in my Aries way) it didn't matter to me much. She was mine and she would be okay. The baby was taken to the children's hospital twenty miles away from where I lay, and I was taken to a public ward where ten other ladies lay in their beds with their brand-new babies in their arms at feeding time.

I lay there feeling lost. Suddenly, the reality of what had happened struck me. I was alone, my daughter was critically ill, and the rest of the world was carrying on as if no crisis had occurred. At the age of nineteen-and-a-half, this was hard to handle.

I lay awake wondering why this had happened to me, to my husband Michael and to my son. It didn't make sense. It was only much later (eleven years later, in fact) that I had a reasonable understanding of why fate had dealt this blow to me.

Katherine was operated on at the children's hospital by an eminent surgeon. He closed the hole in her back and told my husband and me that she would be okay. We were allowed to visit our baby, but not allowed to touch her as she was wired up with tubes and valves and lying in a humidicrib. I gazed at my darling child and felt for her suffering. How I loved my daughter!

Even the nurses decided she was a little angel. One of them said she was the favourite in the hospital.

On the ninth day after her birth, I was excited and thrilled to believe that we were to bring her home the following day. I set aside a cute little outfit full of frills and flounces in which to bring her home. She deserved the best.

I slept quite soundly that night, excited and happy. But at two o'clock in the morning, I sat upright in bed. I had been in a deep sleep and something had stirred within me. I felt a sense of foreboding and looked at the bedside clock. My husband lay sleeping soundly beside me. He was not aware of my feeling. I sat still for the next twenty minutes, waiting for something to happen.

It did.

The phone rang loudly. My husband, startled, reached for the phone. Again, my fears were realised. It was the hospital. Our daughter had died. She had passed over at 2.00 a.m.

I felt her soul pass over our bed; it was an experience I can hardly explain. There was a deep sense of knowing that she was peaceful and strangely still there. This was my very first psychic experience and one that shaped the future of my life.

Yet I still felt smothered by grief and fear. I had, for the first time, come to the realisation that fate can deal a hard hand. I felt somewhat battered and very much at the mercy of a higher force. What kind of force, to cause such anguish? I didn't understand.

My husband took the death badly. He started to drink; he hadn't done so before. My little boy, Mark, couldn't understand why the new baby didn't come to live with us. I grieved very deeply. It seemed the best thing for me to do was to return to my work. Luckily, I loved my job as a teacher. I threw myself into my work and loved my son and my husband and my job. Time went by, and I found myself pregnant again.

This time, I had no sense of foreboding; just a sense of fulfilment and a feeling that God was smiling down upon us once more. It was another baby girl – Jayn, a beautiful gift from God. I thanked him from the bottom of my heart.

I worked long and hard in the classroom and raised my two children. My mind was occupied with work and life and I got on with the business of living.

When my daughter was about nine years old, I was appointed to a school in the western suburbs of Sydney. Here I was to undertake the role of school librarian. This was new to me, as I had no experience. I welcomed the challenge. I was especially happy at the thought of being able to purchase books for the library. The education department had granted quite a large sum of money to the school for this purpose. I prepared myself for the task of selecting the books.

My next psychic awareness came suddenly. I was in the office, waiting for my first class to arrive, when the school cleaner, Carmel, tapped on my window and smiled a warm hello. I waved and smiled and she came in and chatted in her strong Irish brogue. She mentioned that she was going to hold a seance that day after she had finished cleaning. I asked what a seance was – I had no idea. She briefly described how she arranged the letters of the alphabet around a glass and then asked questions. She claimed, to my disbelief, that the glass would move to spell out words. I didn't believe this could be true, so I suggested she get in touch with my daughter. I didn't tell her Katherine's name or give her any other information.

I promptly forgot about our little discussion as I got on with my day. At 3.30 that same afternoon, I saw my Irish friend through the door as she hurried towards me. She appeared to be very excited. I then remembered our morning chat and I asked her how the session went. She handed me a piece of paper. It was folded over and over again. In the middle of the paper was a sentence printed in black ink. It read:

KATHERINE LOUISE – I love you Mum!

I looked at the paper in disbelief. It couldn't be possible. Did I see what I thought I saw? There in black and white was the name of my baby girl who had died eleven years ago. Was this a trick? How did Carmel know my baby's name? No-one at the school even knew I had a baby who had died. I was astonished.

I looked at Carmel. She wanted to know if the message made any sense to me. My eyes widened. I told her that this message was extremely significant and I thanked her for giving it to me. How could I now deal with this experience? Suddenly, I felt very close to my baby Katherine. I again felt her soul, just as I had the night she died. I felt warm and peaceful. I decided I needed to know more. My curiosity had been aroused – well and truly.

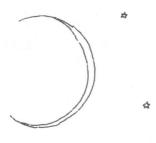

$\mathfrak{M}$y search for meaning

I told Michael what had happened at school that day. I produced the piece of paper. He looked at it, then dismissed it as something that didn't require any time or energy. I was surprised by his reaction, but thought to myself that there was more to my experience that needed to be explained. I realised that Mike could behave in any way he liked regarding my startling evidence – but so could I. I determined to press on with my new-found interest to uncover whatever I could to help me understand what was happening.

The following week I was called to the principal's office. He was an elderly gent, about sixty-five years old and just about to retire. He was a colourful character, full of personality and as determined as an ox to make the most of his last year in teaching. It was rumoured he was having a passionate affair with the infant-school headmistress – an unmarried thirty-eight-year-old woman. I found his sense of humour invigorating and I returned in his banter. He had been easy to work for and I wondered if I should tell him about my message through Carmel. I dismissed the idea quickly as he jolted me back to earth by telling me I should get on with buying books to fill the new library. This seemed a pleasant enough task, so I listened carefully to his suggestion as to how I should tackle the job.

I wandered back to my office thinking I had a rather cushy job, and reached for a telephone directory. I didn't know where to look, so I simply opened up at the 'Warehouses' section and looked through the list until I found a company whose title I felt good about. I decided to give them a call and let them know I had money to spend.

My reception was warm. Sure, they would love to assist me with my task of selecting books for the library. In fact, they would even send out someone to collect me from school and drive me to the warehouse. He would help me with my selection and then deliver me and the goods back to school. This sounded like a good arrangement, so I accepted the offer.

The following week, I was to meet the man who I now know was yet another piece in the jigsaw I was putting together. An elderly man in his seventies, he arrived in an old Ford to collect me from school and escort me to the warehouse. I immediately liked him. He had kind blue eyes and snowy-white hair. There was an air of calmness about him that made me feel safe. We set off in the old car and chugged our way to the warehouse.

As we drove along, my eyes caught sight of a book which was sitting in the open glove box in front of me. The book was called *What is Meditation?* I had heard about meditation, of course, but had no direct experience of it. My life had been too busy to meditate. Anyway, how did one do it? What was it supposed to achieve? I asked Charles, my driver.

He smiled a knowing smile as he heard my questions. 'Are you interested in spiritual matters?' he asked.

'I don't know,' I replied truthfully. 'I do know that I'm interested to find out more about meditation and matters involving the mind,' I said, not sure if I was making sense.

He then proceeded to ask me if I knew anything of life after death. I said I didn't, but then I remembered my experience with Katherine and Carmel. I looked at him. He seemed reassuring. Safe. I believed he would not find it strange if I shared my experience of the seance message with him.

He listened intently, nodding now and then as though he understood. 'You should read a book called *Life After Death* by Arthur Ford,' he said when I finished my story.

By then we had arrived at the warehouse and I went off full of enthusiasm to choose the books and to gather more fuel to feed the fire that was burning within me. At last, I had met another human being who seemed to be 'in the know' about what I had come across so unexpectedly in my life. He didn't think it strange that I showed interest in things I didn't understand. He wanted to help.

I gathered together a load of books and Charles came in a few hours later to collect me. It was cold in the bowels of the warehouse; so cold, in fact, that I began to feel that I was freezing. I pulled my cardigan over my shoulders and buttoned it right up. Still feeling cold, I started to shiver. It was winter and I realised that I was standing in an unheated room with concrete floor and walls. I was grateful when I had at last finished.

Charles led me to the open, spacious office where he indicated that I should sit in a very comfortable leather armchair while he went to collect something. He came back in a few minutes, clutching three books. He handed them to me, smiling benevolently. 'They are for you,' he said.

I looked down at the present. Three brand-new books. A gift from Charles. One was called *Ena Twigg: Medium* by Ena Twigg (with Ruth Hagy Brod). On the cover was a picture of a woman with a very interesting face. The second book was *There is a River* by Tom Sugrue, and the third was *Life After Death* by Arthur Ford. The only one I recognised was the last. I remembered our conversation in the car. I thanked Charles sincerely and we set off for school.

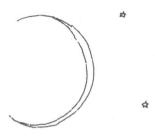

On wings unfolded

I had been unwell since my visit to the warehouse. The coldness that had gone right through me seemed to linger. A week after the visit, I was feverish and felt quite sick. I struggled on at school and at home. One lunchtime, I was so ill at school that I decided to head for a local doctor. Any doctor would do. I waited anxiously until I was called in to see the doctor. He was an elderly Indian man. He examined me and then declared that I had better go straight home to bed; I had developed acute bronchitis. He gave me a repeat prescription for sulphur tablets. I drove home, feeling very dazed and feverish. I collapsed into bed and, exhausted, drifted off to sleep.

Two weeks later I was still sick. I knew that I wasn't making any progress. After a second course of sulphur, I felt worse. I was weak and had lost a lot of weight. I felt guilty that I was not facing up to my responsibilities at home and at work.

One night, while still sick, I was awakened from my sleep by a noise at the side of the bed. I slowly opened my eyes and in a daze I noticed three people standing beside me. Three people? I blinked and looked again. Was I seeing things? One woman had a syringe in her hand. She aimed the needle towards my neck. I felt a pinprick – something like a mosquito bite. I was paralysed with terror and my scream froze in my throat. Not a sound emerged. The other two women just stood smiling peacefully at me. Then they were gone.

I must have been dreaming, I thought, although my neck stung where I had felt the needle going in. Somehow, I was overcome by tiredness and I went off to sleep.

The following morning, I awoke feeling fantastic. Not just better – fantastic! Energy was flowing through me and my head was light and no longer aching. For the first time in a couple of weeks, I was really well. No coughing, no fever, no aches and pains! I remembered my visitors during the night and I accepted that something else weird had happened to me. As far as I was concerned, whatever happened had contributed to my feeling well again. I was thankful and I felt that it didn't need an explanation.

I went back to school again, feeling fit. I was happy. But alas, a few weeks later I had the same symptoms. I knew the bronchitis had returned. I lay in bed yet again, wondering what to do to get better. I thought and thought. The drugs had not really helped me before. My sister had mentioned a chiropractor whom she was visiting for her own problems. I decided to give him a call.

I made an appointment and visited him feeling some trepidation. I didn't really believe in alternative practitioners. They couldn't possibly know about health. Only medical practitioners had all the answers – or so I thought. But as I hadn't got the help I needed so badly, I had to give the chiropractor a try.

After two visits I felt life flowing through me yet again. I stayed religiously on the tablets, vitamins, minerals and herbs that he gave me. I stuck rigidly to the diet he recommended. I felt fine.

However, my health continued to cause me many problems, and so while still in my early thirties I underwent a major operation. During this time I had a most unusual – and profound – out-of-body experience.

I remember flying through a tunnel. This tunnel was very wide and I remember feeling extremely light. I still had my body with me, but I was able to fly. I was extremely calm and contented. I felt a strong and deep sense of fulfilment and I was not at all frightened. I flew onwards, feeling super-happy until suddenly I came to three enormous angels standing in front of me. They were very tall and were most certainly larger than life. They were incredibly beautiful to behold, not only in how they looked, but also in the energy that radiated from them. There seemed to be an iridescence in their forms; both their bodies and their 'souls' radiated warmth and love.

I can clearly remember them gazing at me and one of them, who I 'knew' was seventy feet tall, spoke. 'You can come with us, or you can go back to earth,' she said. 'It's up to you.'

I felt disturbed that I had to make a choice. I desperately wanted to go forward with them but I even more desperately wanted to return to my children and my husband and family on earth. I remember saying 'No, I want to go back and work.'

They all smiled lovingly at me and the 'spokeswoman' said in a firm and loving voice, 'You will know this is not a dream when you wake up by the sign of a cross on the door.'

I awoke quickly, feeling quite well. I also felt comfortably warm all over. When I opened my eyes, the first object I saw was the door of my hospital room. There, on the door, was the shape of a cross. It was made of sunlight. The sunlight was shining through the window which was decorated with pieces of wood in colonial style. The crossing of the wooden pieces formed a cross-like shape and the sun shone through it, reflecting the cross and beaming it onto the door.

I can tell you now that if I was near death with that experience, I would never fear the act of dying. It seemed to be so natural and so loving. But when I returned from the hospital I became quite depressed. I felt lost and alone and I could not understand my situation. I felt as though I were a victim.

I had, in fact, been privy to an amazing event in the visitation of the angels. I know now that the experience was profound, but at the time I was unable to process it. I believe that the magnitude of this experience and the fact that I was then required to deal with everyday life, led to my depression and my feelings of powerlessness.

I found myself in a deep, dark hole from which I did not know how to escape. I wallowed in my misery. Every day I would lie on the lounge in our sunny room and do nothing but stare. Often I would recapture the images of my visit with the angels. Then my aching body would bring me back to earth with a thump. My body was not healing properly and even the loving support I received from my family at this time could not solve the problems I was experiencing. Nothing and no-one could help me come to terms with the reality of my experience with the angels. How could life ever show me the beauty and peace I had experienced during my journey into the life beyond?

It was a time when I wished I had never opened the door to the psychic world.

However, despite six long months of languishing in my depression, my physical body was finally healed. It had responded to the loving care and attention I had received, and now it was up to me to heal my emotional and spiritual bodies …

While in my customary position on the lounge one Sunday morning, I watched a religious program on television. The minister was a peaceful and loving man and his inner strength shone through. Something of my experience with the angels seemed to be evident in the beauty of this man's message. The colours and arrangement of the flowers that adorned his church were truly stunning, and I knew that I had been touched in some way. This was the beginning of my journey back to life and happiness.

I eagerly awaited the hourly program on Sunday mornings. I felt refreshed and my interest in life was restored. My spiritual body soaked up the messages of the sermon and I began to feel a sense of love of creation, and my love of God gave me the strength I needed to climb (even if slowly) out of the depression in which I had been trapped for twelve whole months.

The experience helped me in my work, and gave me a sense of empathy for all those who suffer at the psychological and emotional levels. My encounter with the angels and my emergence from depression was a painful, but significant, moment in my psychic development.

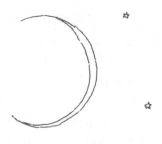

The search
continues

All this time, my interest in spiritual matters grew and grew. I read all I could find on the subject. Strange things occurred. I would walk into a bookshop, as if propelled. I would immediately find myself in front of the most interesting collection of books, all of which were about psychic matters. Charles from the warehouse continued to send books to me through the post. All on psychic matters. All fascinating. I read and read.

Then, one day, I decided to stop. I felt saturated. I felt that I had had enough. I needed to get my mind back to earthly matters. My children demanded my undivided attention. I was moving house. We had bought a large, brand-new home in a lovely suburb. The house was a dream come true. The thought of choosing the fittings and furniture filled me with enthusiasm. I wanted both feet on the ground; I needed to be earthed.

Time marched on, and life was good. The children grew and the house was a delight. I was very contented. I was teaching at a school a long way from home. Again, I was the school librarian. The long drive and the heat became a drain on me, but I wanted to keep going.

One Saturday morning, I was busily cleaning the enormous house of which I was so proud. Suddenly, I felt completely exhausted. I put the vacuum cleaner hose on the floor and collapsed. Michael found me an hour later, still on the floor. I was too tired to move.

I lay in bed all the next day, wondering why I felt so tired. I decided to visit the doctor to see if he could help me understand what was happening to me. Being new to the area, I had no idea who to see so I set off for the local shopping centre where I remembered having seen a doctor's surgery.

I waited – exhausted – in the waiting room, wondering about myself and life. The young doctor took my blood pressure and declared that it was far too high. He wrote out a script for treatment and ordered various tests. I went home to rest.

A week later, my blood pressure was still high. The tablets were not helping as much as they should have been. I stayed away from work and rested. As I lay in my bed, a feeling of darkness overcame me and once again I had the feeling of being lost. I was off track somehow. Was it really physical? Or could it be emotional?

Gradually I became sicker and sicker. A few weeks later, I was in pain. Very bad pain. I went into hospital, where I was seen by a surgeon who decided to operate.

He assured me that after the operation I would be fine. Some kidney stones had lodged somewhere in my body. He would fix the problem.

However, following the operation, I was no better. I was relieved that the stones had been removed, but I still felt dreadful. I went home and lay on the bed. I felt surrounded by doom. Nothing lifted my spirits. I had no energy and life seemed worthless. What was it all about? I didn't care. I just felt like dying.

My husband decided I needed a change. He suggested that we take a drive one Sunday afternoon, so we headed towards the Blue Mountains. I didn't care much where we went. I was still in agony. The pain was everywhere. In my body and in my mind. I was totally resigned to feeling disastrous.

The scenery slipped by. Here and there, I noticed a beautiful group of trees. How green they were! How shady! How pretty! Then some lovely buildings. Zooming past me. Here one minute, gone the next. 'Like life!' I mused.

I started to feel a little more cheerful. We arrived at a picturesque village at the foot of the mountains. I was feeling a lot better. 'Why don't we pay a visit to Fern and Jack?' I asked.

Michael turned the car in the direction of their house. They lived at the top of the mountain. They were home. We could see their car parked outside the house. Fern was a friend whom I had not seen for six years. It would be good to see her again.

She opened the door to our knock. A big smile – really genuine. Arms outstretched. A warm hug. She beckoned us to follow her down the hall. 'I knew you were coming,' she said. 'I told Jack this morning you would be visiting us today.'

Jack approached us from the lounge room. A warm handshake for Mike and a kiss for me. 'That's the truth,' he beamed. I believed him. Fern was a most unusual lady. Nothing about her would surprise me. She was very sincere and had a quality I couldn't quite comprehend. The men started to chat and Fern invited me into the next room, where a table had been set with tea cups and plates. While she pottered about preparing afternoon tea, she looked directly at me and said, 'Would you like a reading?'

I didn't understand. 'What's a reading?' I asked, feeling a bit silly.

'Well, I'll show you,' she said. She walked around the table and took a pack of cards out of a drawer in the sideboard. Then she took out a beautiful, deep blue silk scarf from the same drawer and laid it out on the table. She skilfully shuffled the pack of cards – the biggest cards I had ever seen – and laid them down thoughtfully on the silk scarf.

The cards were unusual. Instead of the numbers and symbols I was accustomed to seeing on cards, they had drawings on them. Beautiful drawings. Some with people and some with animals. I was quite taken.

I still had no idea what to expect. After the cards were laid out, Fern looked straight at me. 'I am going to tell you about yourself,' she said.

She then proceeded to accurately tell me the details of my life over the last six years. I had had no contact with her or her family during that time and I knew she had no earthly way of knowing the things that she was now telling me about my life. She was accurate in every detail. The reading continued for half an hour or so and I was absolutely astounded.

'How do you know these things?' I asked in disbelief.

'Oh, it's easy,' she said, quite overwhelmed by my eager questions. 'Being psychic is simple,' she stated. 'It's all there – you just have to tap into it.'

I left her home that night feeling as though I had stumbled across something totally amazing. I had!

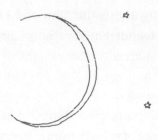

$\mathcal{T}$he search escalates

I began to feel more of a sense of purpose in my life once again. I even began to feel better physically. Fern rang me the following day to tell me the name of a chiropractor she thought I should see. She told me she believed he would help me back to full recovery.

I rang him that evening. He was very busy but he decided to see me the following day, as he knew that I was a genuine case and needed help urgently.

I was anxious as I walked into the tiny fibro home. My knock on the door was answered by a fairly old man with a round body and laughing eyes. He ushered me into the consulting room. I felt frightened. I hated being examined by strangers.

But before long, I felt at ease. There was something unusual about this man. I knew what it was. 'You're psychic,' I said to him.

'Yes, I am,' he replied. It didn't disturb him at all.

He took a magnifying glass and gazed into my eyes. He didn't speak. I wondered what he was thinking. Then he walked to his desk and began to write on a patient record card. He wrote and wrote.

I gazed around the room. On one wall there hung a picture of Jesus Christ. It was the most powerfully beautiful picture of Jesus I had ever seen. Just his face, showing so much love and compassion. I felt a sense of protection come over me and I thought 'Any man who has a picture like that in the room can't be all bad!'

The gentleman promised me that he could make me feel better again. He ordered me to take a mixture of tablets that he handed to me and insisted that I buy a book of exercises that should be done twice daily. I was to eat only those foods listed on the paper he also handed me. I was to see him in three days' time. We made the appointment.

I went home feeling hopeful. Maybe this would help. I hadn't been to school for weeks and I didn't want to return. I just wanted to get better again. Sick leave was a wonderful thing. You had a rest from worries and responsibilities. I made up my mind to enjoy my time off.

I got to work on the diet and exercises and followed them precisely. I swallowed my tablets, feeling better and better each day. I visited the chiropractor twice a week for three months. During this time, he taught me many things. Here was yet another major piece of the jigsaw I was putting together.

On one visit, he invited me to enter a room in the house that was always closed. I had developed quite a rapport with my friend and now began to feel that he was very much a teacher for me. I followed him into the room and once inside felt quite peculiar.

There, on the walls, was a collection of incredibly powerful drawings. They all depicted people whose faces were eerily calm and peaceful. I had had the same sort of feeling when I looked at the face of Jesus in the painting in the consulting room. There were five or six of these drawings, each one with a character of overwhelming beauty. My 'healer' explained that they were his spirit guides. They had been painted by an old man who lived on the south coast. For a small fee, he would tell you who your guides were and then paint them for you.

I had never before encountered the notion of 'spirit guides'. I asked for an explanation. My friend suggested I read more books. He gave me a list of suggested titles. Once more, I was back on the 'trail of knowledge'.

Three months later, I was feeling so well I was almost bursting with good health. I felt enthusiastic for life and especially motivated to discover more spiritual and psychic truths. I made a decision. Deep down, I did not want to continue teaching. I decided to resign. My husband was quite supportive. He just wanted me happy and well.

I gave notice at school with a feeling of great satisfaction. 'Thank goodness,' I thought. But what next? I had too much energy to do just nothing. Housework was fine, but all day, every day, would not be my scene. What do I do next? I wondered.

I decided to enrol at university. I wanted to study psychology – to find out more about the human mind; to see what makes us tick. I enrolled and started the following year. I enjoyed the lectures. The mental stimulation was great. I listened intently to what the lecturers were saying. I took notes. I completed my assignments. I read and read but something was missing. It wasn't complete. The information I was hearing all fitted into little boxes, but I felt there had to be more to it. I didn't know what. I just knew that human beings were far more complex than the picture being painted at university.

I left after six months, but not before a major turning point in my development took place.

One night, I went to bed feeling quite tired. I had completed my first exams that day and I drifted off to sleep, glad that I had less pressure to deal with for a while. At around three o'clock the next morning, I was awoken by something most extraordinary. I opened my eyes because of flashes of fire and light that I saw through the bedroom window. The flashes of colour were quite out of this world and I thought we had been hit by a fire bomb. The whole room lit up. It seemed to go on and on but I didn't feel frightened. I had a strange feeling on my forehead, right between my eyes. Then, suddenly, something lifted. It felt like a physical force just above my eyes. Lights and colour flashed in front of me and my whole head seemed lighter than it had ever been before.

I looked at Michael. He was sound asleep, totally oblivious to what I was experiencing.

The flashes and the sensations continued and I began to think I had had a stroke. I don't drink alcohol much. I don't smoke. I don't take drugs. I knew I was not intoxicated. Flash! Flash! Flash! Then peace! Amazing calm and peace. The room quietened down. All was settled. Enormous peace!

The next morning, I told Michael of my experience. He thought I had been studying too hard.

I rang Fern and told her what had happened. She listened quietly. Then she said quite calmly, 'Your third eye has opened.'

My third eye? What was that? I had never heard of this phenomenon. What was it? She told me to read and recommended a book.

I set off for the bookshop. I found the book easily. In fact, I walked straight towards it. There it was on the shelf. Only one copy left. It was meant for me. I took it and went home to read all I could about it. Yes, it made sense. That had indeed happened to me.

My third eye had opened: my psychic self was born.

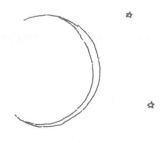

Clairvoyance

A week or so later, I had a dream. It was unlike any dream I had ever had. It was more like a vision.

In this dream-like vision, I saw a classroom. It was a kindergarten room. There were bare floorboards and desks with plastic blocks and wooden toys on them. A strong, beautiful and loving male voice said, 'You are going to become clairvoyant and you are in the kindergarten stage.'

I awoke remembering clearly my experience. That day I was to receive by mail the results of my exams. In the afternoon, I gazed out of the lounge room window and noticed the letterbox. I immediately thought that there was a letter in the box with the results of the exam. I 'saw' the result. I had gained a 'C' pass.

I walked to the box. I opened the lid, and there was the letter. I opened it. I had gained a 'C' pass.

How did I 'know' this? I remembered my vision of the night before. I was clairvoyant and in kindergarten.

Could this be true? Maybe. I would need more proof before I could believe what I had experienced in my dream …

By now, my daughter Jayn was a young adolescent. She was bubbly and full of the joy of life. Her dearest love was horses. She had always loved them. She had her own horse, Laddie. Laddie lived in the five-acre paddock at the rear of our house. He loved Jayn as much as she loved him. She rode him every day. Jayn had gathered around her a circle of friends, all of whom were also horse-lovers and riders. One of those friends was a girl named Heidi. Heidi was a great girl, about eight years older than Jayn and very independent. Jayn had not seen Heidi for a couple of years, as she had gone to Queensland for an extended holiday.

Jayn and I decided to go shopping at the local shopping centre. We loved visiting the mall. It was full of good shops and Jayn and I always had fun together. As we walked along through the crowds, Jayn spotted her friend Heidi heading our way. There was a squeal of delight from them both and questions as to how they both were and what they had been up to over the last couple of years.

As Heidi chatted to Jayn, I began to get some strange impressions in my mind. I heard myself saying, 'You went to Fiji last month, didn't you Heidi?'

She looked at me. 'How did you know?' she asked.

'I don't know,' I replied. 'I just do.'

'You're right,' she said. 'I just got back.'

'And how's Ron?' I asked.

'How do you know about Ron?' Heidi looked stunned.

Somehow, I just knew these things. I went on to tell Heidi a few more things about her life which she said were true. I remembered the words 'You are going to become clairvoyant'. I felt strange. Jayn looked at me as if I had said quite enough. I took the hint. We said goodbye to Heidi and continued on our way.

I told Jayn of my vision. She listened intently. 'Wow, Mum. That's great!'

$\mathcal{T}$urning the gift to health

The phone rang loudly one week later. I picked up the receiver. A woman's voice on the other end asked 'Is that you, Beverley?'

I didn't recognise the voice. 'Yes,' I answered. 'Who's calling?'

She introduced herself to me as Jan. She said that she knew Heidi, who had told her about our meeting at the shopping centre. Would I mind if she paid me a visit? She was going through an unhappy time and needed to talk to someone.

I had no plans for the afternoon, so I agreed that she could visit me that afternoon. I wasn't sure how or if I could be of any help, but I was happy to meet her.

She arrived at the door looking very disturbed. I showed her in and we sat down in the lounge room.

I asked her what the problem was. Before she could answer I found myself telling her what was happening in her life. I talked on and on. She listened and agreed with what I said.

'You are amazing,' she gasped. 'How could you know so much about me?'

'I'm clairvoyant!' I said, feeling satisfied that I must in fact be so.

We talked about her problems and three hours later she left feeling much better. She thanked me for my help and said she'd keep in touch.

At the time this happened, I had enrolled at the School of Natural Therapies. I had decided that university was too contained for me and I needed answers of a different kind. I loved the lectures I was receiving in health, anatomy and physiology. I was particularly enthralled learning about herbs and how they help with the treatment of disease.

I became more and more involved in my search for knowledge and I was very fulfilled. My psychic gift seemed to keep on growing and I found myself talking to the other students about their lives and their growth. They loved it and asked to spend time with me whenever we had a free moment. Eventually, one of the lecturers heard about my gift. She asked me to see her one lunchtime. Why not? I thought. Perhaps it would be fun.

She was a very intuitive lady herself. She asked me for a 'reading'. I 'tuned in' to her, and the door opened to her soul. Information came to me as it always does when I tune in to people: I see, hear and feel truths and guidelines from another realm which will help them along their journey.

I told her about her family and what they were doing. I was accurate. She was thrilled. 'Do you know that you could use this gift to diagnose illnesses?' she queried.

I knew deep down within myself that she was right.

While I was studying at the College of Natural Therapies, I was also studying at the School of Hypnotic Sciences. I needed more and more to know about the power of the mind.

I found hypnosis lectures totally fascinating. I listened and learned. I experimented with my classmates. It was wonderfully rewarding, as well as great fun. Some of these classmates were doctors of medicine. One lady, Rhonda, was an anaesthetist. We practised 'hypnotising' each other. We passed our exam and gained a diploma of Clinical Hypnotherapy.

I hung my diploma proudly on the wall at home. I was ready to see clients.

A friend of mine, Gloria, who I had met through the course had been working as a hypnotherapist for some years and had a very busy practice with her husband. He was also a hypnotherapist. I found them an interesting couple.

One day, Gloria rang me to ask if I would like to see one of her clients. He didn't need hypnosis (she had already seen him professionally); he wanted a reading. She told me that he was prepared to pay for the session and she suggested that I should charge for my services.

I wasn't so sure about that. What if I couldn't 'see' anything for this guy? I decided I should go ahead and not get cold feet at this stage of the game.

The phone rang a day or so later and I heard a very gentle male voice enquire about 'readings'. Was I able to see him, please? We made the arrangements for the following day at my home.

He arrived promptly at two o'clock and I immediately felt that all would go well. I liked him. He was gentle and tall and quite good-looking.

I took him to the lounge room and sat opposite him. I asked him if he had ever had a reading before. He assured me that he had and that he believed I was going to help him. I felt at ease. I needed to know his age. That was all. I then started to tune in to him and discovered that he was sad about the recent ending of a relationship. 'Are you recently divorced?' I enquired. A smile came over him. 'Well, sort of,' he laughed.

In fact, John had recently separated from his partner. I seemed reassured that I was on the right track. I tuned in and more information was given. The truth was that he was feeling very upset by his lost love and wanted to know if I could see the relationship in the future.

I was honest. I told him all that I saw. He was pleased – so pleased that he gladly paid the money. I had had my first professional session.

The next day, I received the biggest and prettiest bunch of flowers I had ever seen. 'With love and gratitude from John' the card read. My first client was obviously happy with my work.

After this, John told other people about the work I was doing. The phone began to ring and appointments were made. John was a television director and had lots of contacts. I became quite busy. I worked from home and began to feel quite fulfilled. I had finished my studies to concentrate more on my work and life was good.

My son, Mark, was finishing high school. He found it difficult to cope with what I was doing professionally. He joked that Mum was 'into voodoo'. But I kept going. Many people passed through my door. One day, I had a call from a woman named Kath. Her twenty-three-year-old daughter Sarah was suffering from lupus disease. She wondered if I could possibly help her.

Sarah had been diagnosed with the disease when she was seventeen years old. She was too sick to work and had never had a job. When Sarah and Kath arrived, I didn't really know how I could help them. I just trusted that I would be directed to give guidance and help.

I asked Sarah to tell me about her health. She described how she felt and what her symptoms were. I asked her about her emotions and her mind. She told me that she felt resigned to a life of pain and discomfort.

I tuned in. I sensed that her body was lacking in certain minerals that could help her. I felt that some of the food she was eating was harmful to her state of health and that other foods not on her diet would be beneficial. So I suggested a plan for her to follow. It included a special diet, and minerals and vitamins as well as herbs. I instinctively felt that if she followed this program she would begin to recover. I gave her hypnotherapy for pain control. She relaxed deeply in the chair. At the end of the session, she said she felt much better – even if it was mind over matter!

One month later, she rang to tell me that her blood test had shown an eighty per cent improvement. I was elated. So was Sarah.

She had decided, because she felt so much better, to look for work and I heard a few months later that she was working as an assistant to an author who lived near her. I derived great satisfaction from Sarah's result. I felt useful. I thought fondly of God and thanked Him for the gift he had given me.

Sarah was a member of the local Catholic Church. She had mentioned her experience with me to a friend who belonged to the same church. Her friend Julie had a five-month-old baby girl, Victoria. Victoria had been born with a birthmark on her buttock. This had become ulcerated. By the time she was five months old, the medical profession had decided they could do nothing to save her life. Gangrene had set in, and the baby was dying.

Julie and her husband, a solicitor, did not really believe in alternative healing, but they had reached the end of the road with conventional medicine. Even the children's hospital specialists had no more answers for poor little Victoria. I was eager to see the baby when Julie rang to arrange the appointment.

The next day, I was busy with the daily grind of washing and house cleaning, when I quite suddenly had an urge to ring John, my television director friend. I was unsure why this need seemed so urgent, but I followed my instinct and rang him. I found myself telling him about the appointment Julie had made with me to see her baby daughter. I somehow felt that I needed reassurance from John that I would be able to guide the parents towards getting Victoria healed.

John listened to me and then said something that quite surprised me. He told me that he was an ordained elder in the Mormon faith and that, for some years, while living in the USA, he had conducted 'healing' services on many occasions. I immediately felt that he should be present when Victoria came to see me. He accepted my invitation and I felt less alone.

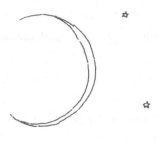

Our first 'healing' session

A few days later, Julie and Victoria arrived at the appointed time. I opened the door to find a young, attractive mother and a beautiful baby girl. Victoria was very quiet. She lay in her mother's arms and looked out at the world through big, round, blue eyes. Julie was distraught. She told John and me that she had come to the end of the road. She believed that her baby would die and she was preparing herself for that eventuality.

I felt deeply moved to take control. I wanted desperately to help this lovely family. I said a silent prayer for guidance. I began to speak. The words came through clearly. Julie was given advice on what to eat as she was still breastfeeding. She listened carefully while John wrote down everything I said. I described the physical problems the baby was having and ordered certain mineral supplements. I then told Julie (through the 'guidance' I was receiving) to mix together certain ingredients which would make an ointment to be applied to the problem area on Victoria's bottom.

I then proceeded to do a 'psychic healing'. I found myself placing outstretched arms over the baby's head and I felt a rush of warm energy surging through my hands. John joined me. He, too, had outstretched arms. I felt the warmth emanating from his hands, even though our fingers were not touching. We both closed our eyes and directed the energy towards the baby. After ten minutes or so, my hands became cooler and I realised that the healing had finished.

Julie took this little display she had just witnessed with great poise. She thanked us both and said she would strictly follow all the instructions I gave. We made an appointment to see the baby in a week's time.

John and I settled down to talk about the session after Julie had left. I told him that I didn't understand what was happening. He assured me that all was fine and he felt sure that the energy was working in a positive way. I hoped so. We decided to meet the following Monday evening at his home. We would discuss his experiences of healing and his philosophy of life.

I began to think I had found a new teacher as well as a new friend. He mentioned that he would also invite a friend of his named Laurie to the meeting. Laurie was a general practitioner and had a great interest in psychic and spiritual healing matters. I looked forward to our evening together.

At John's delightful home, Laurie, John and I talked about our common interests. John told Laurie about the baby and Laurie asked if we could bring her along one night soon so that he could see her condition for himself.

John and I had another session with the baby and I noticed some subtle changes in her wound. It was starting to change colour. While the affected area had been black, it was now turning red. I knew this was good and I told Julie that the blood was starting to flow to the area.

Julie informed us that Victoria had stopped vomiting since our last session, prior to which she had been unable to keep her food down because of a problem with the sphincter muscle. That had settled completely now and Julie was thrilled. At least the baby was getting some nourishment.

I turned my attention to Victoria and suggested some mineral and herbal changes that were now necessary. Once again John took notes. We finished the session with another psychic healing.

On the fourth week after treatment had commenced, I arrived with Julie and her husband and baby at John's house. Laurie was going to be there. He wanted to have a look at the baby. It wasn't long before all five of us were peering over the baby's wound. What a change. The area that had once been totally black and smelly was now soft, new pink skin. In the centre of the wound was a small, moist area. Healing was certainly taking place.

Victoria's parents were delighted with their daughter's progress. I ordered yet more changes in diet and treatment and we all parted that night feeling satisfied that whatever was going on was miraculous.

Eight weeks after the first visit, I told Julie that there was no need for me to see the baby again. She was totally healed. Not even the original birthmark could be seen.

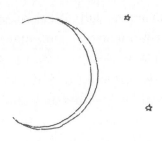

On with the work!

This led me to have enough confidence to believe I was tapping into some force which I certainly didn't understand, but which was obviously loving and good.

My work continued. The phone kept ringing and I was booked for six to eight weeks ahead. I wondered if I would have enough energy to see all the people who wanted my help. I worried how it would be if I was unable to tap into the Source of Truth for my clients. I needn't have worried, for I can honestly say that I have *never* been unable to access information for clients.

I began to feel the strain of my workload. I found it difficult to be a good wife and mother and my children were becoming more and more independent. My husband Michael was very busy with his work and interests and I felt a deep need to have more freedom to explore my spiritual life. I agonised over my life and the choices I could have made in order to find fulfilment. I decided that my new work demanded more of my energy than I could give it while I had the commitment of marriage to deal with. I found myself emotionally drifting further away from my husband and, after great anguish, I decided one day to leave.

I moved into a unit in a nearby suburb. I had never lived in a unit before. I was alone. I felt sad but elated at the thought that I was now totally responsible for myself. I had enough bookings to feel confident that I could pay the rent and I prayed that I would keep on going. I certainly needed an enormous amount of energy and strength to cope with the healing and counselling work I was obliged to undertake.

My children stayed at the family home with their father. Mark was twenty, and Jayn was seventeen. They were sad about the break-up but they were supportive of both Michael and me. Jayn had an evening job at the local skating rink. She would finish work around ten o'clock at night and often would drive over to see me. She had a key to my door, and if I was in bed she would let herself in and come and chat with me while sitting on the bed by my side.

One Wednesday night I went off to bed, exhausted. I easily drifted off to sleep. Some time later I was awakened by a noise at the front door, like someone turning the key. Semi-consciousness told me that it was Jayn coming to visit me. I settled down to a hazy, half-awake state. The next thing I knew, there was a shuffling by my bed and I felt the weight of someone sitting on the bedcovers.

I then felt movement – plonk! plonk! plonk! – across the eiderdown on the bed.

I half opened my eyes. There, through my daze, I saw the outline of my daughter Jayn. A little kitten was scampering over the bed. It was Jason – Jayn's little kitten, only six weeks old. Jayn told me not to wake up. She said she just wanted to see if I was okay. 'Go back to sleep, Mum,' she said. 'I just want to sit with you for a while.' I obeyed, and drifted off once again into a peaceful sleep. I didn't even hear her leave.

The following morning, as I was getting ready to see my first client, I suddenly froze in my tracks. That wasn't Jayn! Jayn had short hair and this girl had long, shoulder-length hair. Jayn had a fringe – this girl did not … That wasn't Jason either! The realisation hit me like lightning. 'How could it be Jason?' I thought. The kitten had died two weeks earlier from feline enteritis. But the girl looked exactly like Jayn. Same size, same colouring, same voice … Not Jayn! My mind convulsed. It was Katherine! My baby girl who had died so many years before, with Jason, our dead kitten!

I immediately rang Jayn. She was on duty at the skating rink. I told her what had happened.

'Mum,' she said. 'You wouldn't believe it. I was at Susan's last night and I was crying because I was thinking of Jason and missing him.'

'Well, dear,' I said, 'don't cry for Jason. He's fine and he's with Katherine.'

Jayn laughed. 'Do you really think so?' she said.

'Yes, I do,' I replied, and hung up.

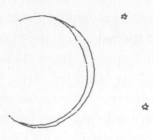

Working with cancer patients

While living at the unit, I found that my work began to change. I was getting more and more clients suffering from cancer. I found my heart reaching out to them. Most of them felt doomed to die. All were receiving conventional medical treatment and many were undergoing chemotherapy and radiation treatment.

I found, in every case, that there were reasons why those patients had cancer. Their first session with me involved a background reading, where I would tune in and look at their life and determine why they needed cancer in their lives. What lessons did they have to learn from this terrible condition?

I would tell them about their lives. This was quite an awesome experience for most of them as they had never before experienced anyone or anything psychic. Often, the reading itself was enough to jar them out of closed or conventional belief systems. The experience helped many to open up to another way of thinking. I pointed out that if they 'needed' disease in their lives, then they also had a choice not to 'need' it.

I saw many people change their attitude to life. Somehow they were able to get in touch with their higher selves. I told them of diet, herbs, vitamins and minerals and, above all, positive thinking.

One case that I remember quite clearly was that of a twenty-three-year-old man who had lymphoma and leukemia. His father rang me one afternoon to tell me about his son, Andrew, who was unable to walk without the aid of a walking frame. He had been told that he had only six months to live. The father was naturally very upset about his son's condition. He asked me to visit Andrew at their home because the boy was unable to travel.

John and I set off the following day. We met Andrew, who was about six feet tall, extremely thin and very gaunt and pale. He was shuffling along with a walking frame in his rather large and very busy-looking bedroom.

Andrew plonked himself on the bed and looked up at us feebly. I felt great compassion for this young man who should have been bursting with life. He told us that he had been given six months to live by the hospital specialists. 'They're not God,' I thought to myself. 'How can they say that?' I didn't voice my thoughts.

I proceeded to do a reading for Andrew. I told him what his ambitions were and I told him of his hopes and dreams. He seemed surprised and agreed that I was correct. He had, in fact, hoped to have a rock 'n' roll band and had wanted to tour the country with them. I said there was no reason he couldn't fulfil his dreams.

He looked at me disbelievingly. I continued. I told him of events in his past which had an effect on his psyche and which needed to be dealt with mentally and emotionally before he could get well again. He knew what I was saying. He started to respond with enthusiasm. He asked me questions about his life, his family, his friends. We worked through a lot of issues that had been troubling him.

Then I tuned in to his physical state. I listed many herbs, minerals and vitamins that I knew would help the body gain strength and get well again. I gave him a list of foods he should eat and just as many foods he should not eat. He promised me that he would follow my advice as he had nothing to lose. John and I did a psychic healing. As I did with all my patients, I insisted that he should continue with the conventional medical treatment he was receiving.

Six weeks later, Andrew showed no signs of leukemia or lymphoma. Even after seven years there is still no sign of cancer. I found many patients responded in a similar way. I saw many people with brain tumours, breast cancer, bowel cancer, liver cancer, leukemia and other forms of cancer. I didn't do the work on them. They did.

I just showed them another way.

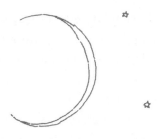

Other spheres of existence

There are many different ways of encountering other spheres of existence, and some of these I have already shared with you. But there have been occasions throughout my psychic journey on which I have consciously set out to explore other means of communication, or in which departed souls and others from these spheres have made contact with me …

After I had begun to develop psychically, I went through a period of experimentation in my quest to seek more answers, and so I decided to investigate astral travelling. In my reading about this interesting subject, I discovered that astral travel is available to all of us and that most of us engage in this activity while we are asleep. While the physical body is at rest, the soul floats to the astral plane.

The physical body is anchored to the astral body by the Silver Cord which prevents the soul from becoming lost. While some people with evolved souls do recollect their astral journeyings, most people forget their experiences once the physical body awakes.

I do not recommend that you, the reader, imitate what I did as you may be at an entirely different level of your own development and I believe we should be very wary of anything we don't fully understand. However, I'll tell you what I did.

I telephoned my sister, Sue, and told her that I hoped she would help me to know more about astral travelling. Sue agreed. I told her of my plan. She thought it might be interesting and felt that all would be quite safe.

My plan was to travel astrally to visit her. I would ring her half an hour later to tell her what I had seen while visiting her. Sue lived about fifteen miles from where I lived at the time. I sat comfortably in the armchair in the lounge room. I then willed myself to visit my sister. I remember 'flying' straight to her house. I don't remember seeing anything at all between her home and my own. In an instant I was flying above her. She was standing at her laundry sink. I looked down into the water. Soaking in the sink was a red article of clothing. Sue then walked out to the clothes line in her backyard. I followed her. Outside in the garden I could see her two children, Bertie and Alice. They were squealing happily, chasing their little black fluffy dog. The dog was yelping and barking. It was obviously enjoying the fun. Sue hung the washing on the line.

Next, the dog took off inside the house through the open back door. It ran in through the laundry to the kitchen. The two children both rushed in, screaming excitedly, chasing the dog. Sue saw them all heading into the house and joined in the chase. I flew above her. She raced into the kitchen, and as she did so, I saw her bump her hip on the corner of the kitchen table as she slipped on the floor. 'Ouch!' I thought. 'I bet that hurt.'

The dog and the kids were shooed outside and Sue sat down rubbing her sore hip. I willed myself to return home. I opened my eyes. I was safe and sound in my armchair, feeling quite refreshed and relaxed. I was also feeling very excited. Had what I saw really happened? I went to the phone. It was exactly twenty minutes since I had last spoken with Sue. She picked up the receiver and I remember her saying 'Well, what happened?' I told her every detail of the story of my visit to her.

She was flabbergasted. 'That's exactly what happened!' she said. 'My hip is really sore.' We both laughed and I wondered how I could integrate this experience into my everyday world.

Over the years, I have conducted readings for people who were grieving for loved ones. Many had no intention of spending the session talking about their grief. However, during the session I have been informed often by the departed soul that the client needed help to handle their sadness. Often, the spirit on the other side had a message for the client.

One case I recall vividly was that of a woman who visited me just after I had begun to see clients. She walked down the stairs that led to the lounge room of our split-level home. As I watched her walking down the stairs, I 'saw' the spirit of a baby sitting just above her shoulder. The baby girl was about eighteen months old. I looked at my client and instinctively felt that I must tell her what I saw.

'Did you lose a baby about eighteen months ago?' I asked.

She looked surprised. Then she burst into tears. 'Yes,' she said. 'My baby girl died eighteen months ago.'

'Well, don't be so upset,' I said. 'She is with you now.'

I went on to describe the baby's physical condition that had led to her death. The mother confirmed that this was correct. We talked about the fact that the little girl was with the mother, in spirit, and that all was well. Many tears later, the woman thanked me for allowing her to deal with the death of her daughter in this way.

Another experience of dealing with a departed soul occurred some years later. By then I had had a lot more experience in dealing with psychic events, and nothing really surprised me. I had moved into a flat in a cosmo-politan beach-side suburb. I was quite content with my life and I poured all my time and energy into my psychic work.

One day, my friends Ross and Anne came to visit me at my flat. Ross is a cardiologist and a very brilliant man. His wife Anne, whom I had met teaching, is my dearest and closest friend. They were just beginning to show an interest in the work I was doing, although they didn't

really understand what it was all about. Ross was inquisi-
tive. He had very strict scientific views about life and the
universe and he wasn't really looking to change them.
However, he did have an open mind. That was all that
was required if he was to find out more about the work I
was doing.

On this Saturday afternoon, he asked me to 'look' into
one of his patients. He told me the man's name and age.
That was all I needed. I tuned in. I immediately felt that
he was no longer an earthly body. Ross agreed. 'Tell me
what he died from.'

I described (psychically, of course) the man's heart
condition and I remember saying that there was a part of
his body that had gone black some time before his death.
Ross nodded. It was the toe. He had developed gangrene
as a result of his heart condition. I also told Ross where
the patient had lived. Again, Ross agreed.

With the man's spirit passing on information, I went on
to tell Ross how the patient had been very upset before
he died. He was disturbed because he knew that
a 'lady wearing a yellow uniform' was rifling through
his personal belongings in his bedside cupboard. She
had stolen some money. Ross said that the kitchen
staff wore yellow uniforms, and after I described a
woman in detail he promised to investigate the matter
further.

The following week I visited Anne and Ross in their
unit near the busy teaching hospital where Ross worked.
He told me that the hospital had had other reports about
the kitchen hand described by the spirit of the patient a

week earlier. She had been dismissed by the hospital following an investigation of other complaints.

Ross began to believe that there was more to life than just science, especially when strange things began to occur at the flat he shared with Anne and their two children.

Anne had been noticing some unusual noises in the flat while Ross was away at work, noises that could not easily be described. One day, she noticed that the bust of Hippocrates was not in its usual spot on the shelf high above Ross's desk in the study. She knew she hadn't moved it. Her children were only babies, so they hadn't moved it. Ross definitely had not moved it. No visitors had been present in their home and they had not been burgled.

They called me to investigate. I went into the room. I immediately felt the presence of a woman about twenty-eight years old. I said she died of a heart condition and had been operated on a few weeks before her death. I described a metal valve that had been implanted in her heart in the hope of saving her from further heart problems. I gave her first name. I described her condition, and added that she had had two children, a boy and a girl. I gave their ages.

Ross remembered the case. I told him the woman was concerned about her son. Apparently he had been having great trouble coming to terms with her death. His little sister had coped better. I relayed to Ross some things the mother wanted her little boy to know. These were to help him with his grief. The mother admitted to me (in spirit form) that she had moved the bust of Hippocrates to gain attention so that her messages could be received. I felt satisfied that the message was given, and I knew Ross began to ponder more and more.

Certainly Anne was by now convinced that there is so much more than we will ever know.

There have been other cases of contact with souls who have wanted to 'tell' their loved ones still on earth about where to find certain items for the settlement of wills, and so on. Some souls also want to tell their family not to grieve for them because they are in fact extremely happy on the 'Other Side'.

Some souls simply want to tell what happened to them at the scene of their death. I remember one case of this happening during a reading I gave to a woman whose brother had died a few weeks before our session.

She had booked to see me not because of her brother's death, but because she was seeking guidance and direction in her life. She thought spiritual guidance might provide her with some help. After our session had commenced, I was very aware of the spirit of a young man with her. I saw clearly this young man, who seemed insistent that I acknowledge him and listen to what he wanted me to hear. I stopped talking and turned my attention towards him. He wanted his sister to see through his eyes what had happened to him.

I relayed the events as he told them to me. He said that he had had an argument with his girlfriend. He loved her very much, and wanted to marry her. Following the argument, he left her home and got on his motorbike. He zoomed off into the pouring rain, hardly able to see where he was going. As he thought about the argument he drove faster and faster. Suddenly his bike skidded on an object on the road. Still on the bike, he was headed for a telegraph pole. Nothing could stop the collision. He felt nothing. He saw himself floating above his body, which was lying on the side of the road. He saw a crowd of people gather around the body, and he lingered over the scene. He knew he was dead as he saw himself being placed into the ambulance.

He told me to tell his sister he loved his girlfriend and he wanted her to get on with her life and marry someone else. He spoke to me about his favourite coat, a checked coat hanging in his father's wardrobe. His parents had separated when he was young and he had often stayed with his dad. He sent his love to his sister and wished her happiness.

My client was in tears as she listened. I felt the love between them. She said she knew the coat he had talked about. She thanked me for helping her. I felt privileged that I was able to be used as an instrument of communication in this way.

Being a psychic means that from time to time I see a ghost. I do not usually consciously look for them but sometimes I see them whether I like it or not.

One of my friends, Diane, and I had decided to attend a lecture together in the country. We were booked in to stay in a country motel. Across the road from the motel was a lovely old restaurant. The restaurant had been restored from its original state and was a truly charming old heritage-listed building. We decided to dine there on the Saturday evening. At dinner, Diane and I chatted away about the day's lecture, which was about psychic phenomena.

I was happily relaxed. After our meal, we returned to sit in the lounge area facing a blazing log fire. We were very comfortable, relaxing by the dancing flames, when I became aware of a presence in the room. There were no other guests in the lounge area, but I could clearly see a little girl about eighteen months of age. She was crying and appeared to me in a four-poster cot. I became aware that she was distressed because she was having difficulty breathing. The image faded and the crying stopped.

I told Diane what I had just experienced. She listened eagerly. A few moments later, the maître d' appeared. He was a very matter-of-fact type of person who enquired as to whether we would like a drink. Diane exclaimed that we would like a glass of wine and then she proceeded to ask (much to my surprise) whether or not the restaurant was known to have any ghosts.

A big smile crossed the waiter's lips. He seemed thrilled with the question. He eagerly proceeded to tell us the story of the little girl who had died in the building, in fact in that very room, over one hundred years before. She was the eighteen-month-old daughter of the owner of the house which, at the time, had been a coach stop for the Cobb and Co coaches as they travelled from Sydney to Melbourne with deliveries. The little girl had died of asphyxiation, probably caused by an asthma attack.

Diane looked at me and I looked knowingly back at

her. We both looked at the waiter and neither one dared volunteer what had just taken place!

I remember another such experience when I was in Dover, England. Bruce and I had decided to stay in an old bed and breakfast hotel, while awaiting the ferry that would take us to Calais in France the following day. When we checked in, the young woman at the desk informed us that there was only one room available. This was on the third floor at the top of a very steep and narrow flight of stairs.

I shuddered at the thought of climbing stairs. (I am terrified of heights and turn to jelly at the thought of climbing anything over two feet off the ground!) I cringed and gave a pleading look to Bruce. He quickly understood my terror and calmly asked if there was any other room available. After some deliberation (I soon learned why!), the young woman decided that we could have a room on the first floor which had just suddenly become available. I was so relieved, even more so when we entered the room and I saw that it was clean and sparsely, but suitably, decorated. This would certainly do for the night.

I unpacked a few items of clothing and fell, exhausted, onto the bed. Bruce has much more stamina than I, and decided to go off and explore the sights of Dover while his wife snoozed the afternoon away. I fell exhausted into a deep sleep. Suddenly, I became aware that Bruce was sitting on the end of my bed. I opened one eye to verify that the heavy body at the end of the bed was, in fact, Bruce. To my complete dismay I discovered that it was not.

I saw a tall, thin man gazing at me with grey, kind-looking eyes. He seemed very peaceful; he also 'felt' peaceful. I knew I was completely safe with him. He was dressed in nineteenth-century costume. He wore a long jacket which was loose and grey-coloured. His hat was tall and black, and decorated on the side with a black band and a silver square buckle. This matched the shoes which I glimpsed at the end of his stockinged feet.

I battled with the reality that I was dealing with someone or some thing from another sphere. I quietly asked him his name. In a very gentle, even tone, he told me that his name was Alfred McKnee and that he had been a sea captain on a sailing vessel which had overturned and sunk in rough seas in the English Channel. He explained that this occurred in 1857 and that he had drowned while trying to save the life of the eleven-year-old cabin boy. He himself had come from apple-growing country in Kent, where his family had apple orchards. He loved apple cider, which he made himself. He told me of drinking the ale in glass mugs on board the ship.

He said that the bedroom we were now in was his room and he stayed there often before sailing across the Channel. I asked him if he minded our being in his room. He gave me a slight smile, nodded his head, and vanished before my eyes. I took this to mean we were welcome to stay overnight in his room.

I did not see him again during the rest of our stay there, and I happily shared my experience with Bruce when he returned from his afternoon walk. We decided not to mention the events of the day to the landlord, as I was not sure whether we would be believed, but somehow I think they knew. Why else would they have not offered us the room on the first floor?

The events of the day were vividly brought back to my consciousness a month or so later. We were travelling through the English countryside by train, having spent a fabulous few weeks touring around Europe. As I gazed out of the window at the scenery rushing by, I noticed apple orchards – green and red and in full bloom. The sight was delightful. The train pulled in to the station and a big sign read 'Welcome to Kent'. I had had no idea that Kent was apple-growing country before my friend Alfred had visited me that dull afternoon in Dover.

Part two

Who are we?

My theoretical framework

*T*hus far, my life had been a series of extraordinary events all leading to a new discovery of self and hopefully to a better understanding of humanity and our role in the universe. I feel that every event that occurs in life is lending weight to our growth – spiritually, physically and emotionally.

The lessons we have to learn are often painful and it does take a lot of courage to be able to survive and to reap the benefits of understanding and growth. It is always tempting to take the easy way out, to run away rather than to stay on and battle through the problems that arise. But in order to grow, we must!

We need perspective. We must be able to rise above ourselves and look down on what is happening to us just as one does in an out-of-body experience. To be able to view our own life objectively rather than subjectively is the greatest skill we can learn. If we couple this with the belief that God loves us and is a kind and caring being, then we truly have a valuable instrument to use when we need it.

We must develop a sense of wonder about our own self and a sense of love and self-respect. By this I don't mean that our own needs and desires should come before those of everyone else. Far from being a selfish notion, I believe that a concept of our own uniqueness is vital to achieve so that we can respect others who share our world. If we love and respect ourselves, we can then broaden our perspective by extending this unconditional love to other human beings. Race, colour and religion are not barriers to loving unconditionally. We are part of a wondrous creation at the centre of which is our God. We share this wonder with all living things, every one of which is a part of God and is wondrous in itself.

Within this concept there is a need to view our planet as part of a much wider world, all of which God has created. Our earth is only a minute part of the universe, yet we are infinitely important to our creator. We must all work to restore love and harmony between ourselves, and to foster love and respect for all creation.

We attract similar souls; teachers are brought forward to help us on our journey. Often they do not appear in the guise we expect them ...

From my own search for knowledge, meaning and truth, and through my reading, my contact with others, and especially my spiritual mentors and teachers, I have put together a way of understanding who we are as human (physical and spiritual) beings. It is this theory that underlies my work as a psychic and healer.

It is these ideas that are the subject of this part of the book.

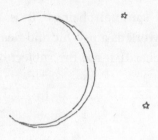

Our physical body

It is as essential to take care of our bodies as it is to look after the psychological and spiritual aspects of our being. We must be conscious of the fact that our body is the result not only of our genetic inheritance, but also of what we feed it and how we use it.

Diet is of the utmost importance. We each must take responsibility for what we eat. If we pause to take stock of our eating habits, then we will choose those foods that assist our body rather than hinder it. If we treat our body as a machine that needs careful and continual mainten-ance then perhaps we will start to develop a healthy respect for how we feed it.

In general, I believe our body will perform better if we feed it fresh fruits and vegetables. Where possible, I believe that whole fruits and vegetables are better than those peeled and squeezed. I also believe that if we can avoid cooking vegetables we will gain more of the nutrients they can provide. If cooked vegetables are preferred, then steaming or microwaving seem to be the least destructive cooking methods. It is also the case that many of the nutrients in fruits and vegetables are found in the skin, and therefore we should try to avoid peeling our food. Of course, many of our fine foods are sprayed with pesticides so we must be careful to wash our food thoroughly if we don't grow it ourselves.

We should try to eliminate all unnecessary fats, salts and sugars from our diet. These tend to add to our health problems in many cases and can be the cause of imbalance and disharmony. It is important that we check with our doctor if we decide to make any major changes to our eating habits, and those people on special medical diets must adhere strictly to their doctor's advice. Choosing fresh, healthy foods and making sure we drink lots of fluids will make us feel better. Probably the best fluid intake is purified water with a squeeze of lemon in it. We should try to have at least six to eight glasses of water a day. I have discovered that the lemon is one of nature's most wonderful foods. It has cleansing, purifying qualities, and our skin and general vitality will benefit if we use lemon daily. It is important that we eat food from the various food groups in order to have a healthy body: we all need protein, carbohydrates, dairy products, legumes, fruits, vegetables, lentils, nuts and water, daily.

If we are vigilant in maintaining a healthy diet, then our body will respond positively. We should remember that the human body has the innate ability to heal itself. It also has the capacity to maintain itself if we feed it the correct nutrients. If we look after our body, it will look after us!

It is also important that we exercise if we want to keep healthy and fit. I personally believe that exercise should be gentle rather than strenuous and I recommend the use of an exercise bike for people who aren't able to get out for walks and gentle runs. Swimming and tennis can provide good exercise as well as enjoyment. If we exercise in moderation – as with most things in life – we'll find a balance that rewards our body and refreshes our mind.

Some other requirements for a well-balanced and healthy body are fresh air, adequate rest, sleep and relaxation. Fresh air is required to keep an adequate supply of oxygen in our body. These days it may not be so easy to find pure fresh air as we have managed, unfortunately, to pollute our atmosphere with the use of too many chemicals. It is up to us to respect our environment and to try to keep it as natural and pollutant-free as possible. We must also, from time to time, visit places of nature that are relatively free of pollutants. The bushland and coastal waters in many areas are often the safest places to get some fresh air into our lungs. Remember, then, that just as we must eat correctly, so we must also exercise well and enjoy plenty of fresh air.

In order to keep the balance of a healthy body, mind and soul, we must make sure we get enough sleep. Sleep is vital to repair and replace cells. We must also sleep to balance our minds. In sleep, we deal with issues that arise from our emotional and spiritual bodies. It is important to know just how much sleep our body requires and it is our duty to give ourselves the amount of sleep our body needs.

In our stressful society we often forget to take time to relax. If we don't get enough relaxation, stress can interfere with the normal way in which our bodies function and ill-health can result. We should make a habit of taking some form of relaxation every day. Meditation techniques can help us to relax, and will greatly assist our physical, psychological and spiritual bodies. Listening to music or pursuing a favourite hobby may work best. Whatever method we choose to help us relax, we must make sure we engage in it on a daily basis.

If we have a healthy body and mind, then we will be in a position to have a clear and free spiritual body. Let's now have a closer look at our psychological body.

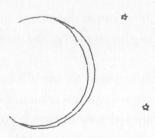

Our psychological body

As I have mentioned, we are made up of a psychological self as well as a physical self. Our psychological self is just as important to our wellbeing as our physical self, if not more important.

Some people suffer enormously in life because they lack an understanding of how to balance themselves psychologically. Perhaps this simple philosophy might assist you if you are looking for guidance on how to balance yourself.

I believe that we humans belong to one big family. We are all brothers and sisters, despite gender, social status, colour, race and creed. We have all been created by the One Force. This force I call God. God created us all equally in the beginning. At some point, we were all simply sparks of energy. We were allowed and assisted to grow, develop and evolve according to our own individual desire to utilise this self-energy. Some of us chose to develop quickly, some slowly, and some chose to stagnate. This same choice is still ours today. The existence that we are now experiencing in this life is our own. We can choose to do with it what we want.

I believe we are just passing through during our life on earth. Where are we going? you might ask. I believe we are journeying through eternity to our ultimate desti-nation. This is to be at one with God, our creator. To achieve this, we reincarnate our earthly bodies. We choose our bodies as we choose our clothing. They are simply outer covers for our souls. The soul continues on with our journey after the body dies.

Our physical body is a reflection of what first occurs in our psychological body. I believe that disease manifests itself in the physical body only *after* it has been born in the psychological. As I will explain later, some psychics can 'see' oncoming disease of the physical body by first seeing it in the psychic body of the individual. When disease is already present in the physical body, psychics can sometimes see it through the ethereal body, or aura of the person concerned.

It is important, therefore, to keep ourselves as psychologically healthy as possible. I have found that people suffering from certain illnesses have a tendency to be the same personality types. For example, through my own work of dealing with physically sick people, I have noticed that cancer patients have most commonly a personality that tends to internalise feelings. A lot of cancer patients are very 'deep' people who like to keep their thoughts and feelings to themselves. I have seen this over and over again when doing my initial reading. I tell them this and ask them to open up and work with their angers, fears and frustrations. This, I believe, is part of the cure and is as important as diet, herbs or drug therapy.

I once worked with Noni Hazlehurst, one of Australia's best-known movie and theatrical actors. She is a most interesting person. She came to see me one afternoon for a reading. She was suffering from abnormal cervical cells and smear tests showed a worsening of the condition every three months.

Noni was seeing a naturopath, receiving dietary advice and medication. I also worked long and hard with her, especially on her psychological body. We discussed her innermost feelings with regard to many close relationships in her life and we cleared away a lot of emotional debris. She did the work and has benefited by having a clean bill of health since that time. She is also the proud mother of two beautiful sons, despite the fact that the doctors felt she needed to undergo a total hysterectomy.

This is a case of a patient who needed to balance her psychological state before she could respond wholly to treatment. I believe this element is essential for health and wellbeing, whether a patient is on conventional medical treatment or alternative treatment or a combination of both. This means we all have a duty and a responsibility to ourselves to make sure we externalise our negative thoughts and emotions. We must not carry around anger, hatred, fear or frustration. We must do the best we can to release these feelings. To achieve this, we might find it easier to enlist the help of a trusted friend, family member or even a therapist.

Once our psychological self is in balance, then we can feel harmony throughout our entire being and this is when true healing can take place.

Our spiritual body

Our spiritual body houses our 'overself'. It is in this body that the true self lives. Our spiritual self is the one that powers our being and keeps us eternally alive. Some people need to relate to themselves spiritually and so they seek to discover their spiritual self. Others have no need for this as they are not as spiritually 'aware' and are 'younger' souls. As we journey through eternity from one reincarnation to another, we awaken more and more of our spiritual selves.

We all have guides which are similar to the guardian angels referred to in the Bible. These guides can be in the form of souls who are ancient and wise, or they can be friends or relatives of ours. These souls are people who have passed over to the next plane, but who wish to protect and guide loved ones on earth.

To know that we are not truly alone in life can give us a sense of inner peace. We have loving forces around us even if we are blind to their love and caring. They are benevolent forces who would never interfere with our thoughts, decisions and directions, but who are there if we wish to recognise them. I will never forget an experience I once had in my early days of psychic development which was my very first introduction to this idea of guides.

My friend Maureen had met a woman who had been a member of the congregation of a spiritual church. The woman had told Maureen about many of the marvellous experiences she had had while belonging to the church group. Maureen was interested to visit such a church to find out for herself whether or not such events could really take place. I accompanied her on a bright, sunny day, not knowing what to expect.

I was greeted at the door of the church, along with all the other members of the congregation, by the reverend. She was a very pretty woman who appeared to be in her early forties. She was adorned with lots of heavy jewellery, and looked like any other suburban housewife. The reverend greeted me with a warm hug and a kiss on the cheek. She then held my hands and gazed deeply into my eyes.

'You have with you in spirit,' she said, 'a little girl who died of heart failure. She is almost fourteen years old and her name is Katherine.'

I could not believe my ears. Had I heard correctly? She told me that Katherine loved me very much; that I am her mother and my daughter was, in fact, very peaceful and happy. I was dumbfounded. I looked at my friend and wondered what I had encountered.

We moved into the church and settled down on a seat facing the front. A small group of about thirty people was seated and awaiting the service. After some very moving singing, everyone was in the mood for things to happen.

Our reverend decided that we would all be introduced individually to our spirit guides. I pondered the concept of guides, but after my greeting at the church door I was ready for anything.

One by one, each member of the congregation was called up to the front of the building. We were asked in turn to stand facing the back of the church. We stood in front of a bare wall, while the reverend and three of her helpers (in earthly bodies!) stood at the back of the church and gazed intently at something they appeared to see behind each one of us.

When my turn came, I stood looking at the women who were going to connect me with my guides. In unison, I heard all four of them call out 'Ron'. The reverend then went on to explain that Ron was a tall, thin and very beautiful-looking male with a gentle face. He had passed over to the other side in an accident in which his legs were badly hurt. The reverend assured me that he was very caring and loving and had been assigned to watch over me and help me in my quest for higher knowledge. I quietly thanked the reverend and her helpers and returned to my seat in the second row to watch, with great interest, the rest of the proceedings.

I can honestly say that for each person at the front of the church, the group of psychics at the back of the building called out a different name *in unison*. It is easy to be sceptical and think that perhaps somehow the whole scene had been orchestrated, but I can tell you that most of the congregation were first-timers to this church. Also, the way in which certain information about each individual was revealed would have made it impossible for any deceptive means to be employed.

I was absolutely astounded by my experience, as were the other people who were in attendance that day. We chatted together after the service. More questions were left unanswered than were answered by this enlightening experience.

When reading for a client I have often seen guides who are totally unknown to them. However, in many sessions I have seen a spirit guide who I describe to the client – often giving a name to the spirit – and who my client immediately recognises.

I remember the case of Desiree. When she first visited me for a reading, she had just completed her Bachelor of Arts degree. She wanted to know about her future direction. I remember telling her that she would travel overseas and that she would stay there for at least three years. At that time in her life, Desiree had no plans to travel. I also could see that she would become quite ill while away. I assured her that she would recover and I advised her to stay overseas because she would get very reliable medical care there.

Desiree returned to see me three years later. She had, in fact, travelled since her previous visit to me. While living in Italy, she had contracted meningitis. She had been very ill and did consider returning to Australia. She remembered the message of her reading to stay overseas. She decided to stay and received expert help in an Italian hospital. She was grateful for the psychic advice given at our first session. She now wanted to see what else fate might have had in store for her.

I concentrated on tuning in to her. I saw a guide standing beside her. I described a man who appeared to be a very imposing figure. He was of Tibetan origin. I asked him his name. Immediately I was told that he was called 'Aranuk'. He explained to me that he had been a Tibetan monk while alive on earth. He had had the unpleasant duty of determining whether children were fit enough to survive after birth in his country of Tibet. His task was to place the newborn infant in the freezing cold water of the mountain stream and if they survived they were fit enough to endure a very hazardous lifestyle. Aranuk claimed that he found this duty very disturbing and it upset him to have to perform it. However, it was a very important task and he had had no choice, as a monk, but to perform it. He described to me his role as a guide for Desiree. He gave some advice about her future.

I delivered these messages to her and she sat quietly and listened to all that I said. When Aranuk had left our presence and returned to the Great Beyond, Desiree announced with great excitement that she found the session amazing. She told me that she had been reading a book that she had purchased while visiting Tibet. The book told the story of a Tibetan monk who had lived in Tibet in the thirteenth century. It was a true account of the life of the monk. She was completely overwhelmed when she told me the name of the monk was Aranuk!

I assured her that I had never read the story of Aranuk. She told me she would have been surprised if I had, because the book of his life was purchased in Tibet and was not released for publication in Australia. The story of Aranuk, according to the book, did in fact endorse the story that I had told Desiree about his role in bathing the children in the mountain streams.

Both Desiree and I began to consider what we had experienced in her session. I have concluded that her guide was teaching her through the book she read and this was confirmed by the reading she had with me.

Our ethereal body

Beyond our physical, psychological and spiritual bodies is an ethereal body. This is an imprint of the physical body. It is the same size and shape as the physical body but it is different in that it has no texture or weight and is made up of a bluish-grey substance. When people see ghosts they are seeing the imprint or ethereal body of the person who has passed on to another plane.

The ethereal body is housed between the physical body and the aura. Within the ethereal body is a soul. When the physical body dies, the soul goes on. It travels on to other 'planes'. The plane it travels to depends very much upon the evolution of the soul. Each soul is an individual and is therefore at its own level of evolution. When I or another psychic tunes in to a person, we are tuning in to the ethereal body and soul of the person. This is where the 'aura' of the person may be seen.

An aura is an electrical field around every human being. A psychic can read auras by their different colours. The different colours show different aspects of the person. Whenever I see a royal blue aura, I feel that the person is quite well, having undergone a healing of either a physical or a spiritual nature. A pink aura tells me that the person is surrounded by love, but may not be aware of this. A green aura shows a calm person and one who is sometimes dealing (deep down) with jealousy and envy. White light in the aura shows a soul that is highly evolved and capable of unconditional love. An orange aura indicates a very active and academic mind; perhaps that of someone who is studying all the time. Dark colours usually represent illness or disease in the physical body. A further investigation with the person would reveal more details.

Of course, there are various shades in between and some auras are a mixture of many different colours. I do not read auras primarily when doing a reading, but I will often notice an aura during the course of a session.

I believe that if we are aware of keeping a balance of our spiritual selves, then we can avoid illness and disease. As I have mentioned, disease can show up in the aura of a person before it manifests itself in the physical body. If it can be worked on in the spiritual body, then the disease in the physical body may never manifest itself. It is possible to intercept physical disease! This is why meditation is important. We can meditate in different ways. I believe that we can meditate as we go about our daily tasks. Much depends on our attitudes and our state of mind, for human beings are more than just the physical body that we can see and touch and hear. We have an 'electrical' self that forms our ethereal body. When we are in harmony with ourselves, the ethereal body 'glows'. It is important that the ethereal body is in good shape so that we can keep to optimum levels of health and wellbeing.

Part three

Channelling – Anna Maree

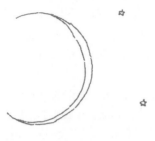

*C*hannelling is a form of communication between human and spirit forms. It is not the only way in which we can receive information from other realms, but it is a more well-known form of contact between our different states of being.

One of the most interesting phases of my exploration into the psychic world commenced when I 'met' one of my spiritual guides, Anna Maree, through channelling. Anna Maree communicated through me whilst I was in a state of deep relaxation. This is how our sessions with Anna Maree began ...

Once a week, over twelve months, I would meet with my two good friends, John and Laurie, who I introduced you to in Part 1. John, Laurie and I are each on our own spiritual journey for truth and growth. Our meetings were held in the evening at John's friendly, comfortable home. We were all novices at this form of learning. We formed a circle by holding hands around a table and I would go into a light trance. It was not something I wanted desperately to explore; it simply seemed to happen. At the time of our experimenting, it occurred very naturally. I found myself very relaxed and in this state of deep relaxation I would begin to talk, allowing the words to flow *through* me rather than consciously *from* me.

It was quite a strange experience but one that I have found beneficial in many ways. I think it helped me to realise that humans do not operate solely on an earthly plane. In other words, I believe we are never *truly* alone. This concept is very comforting, especially in times of sadness and depression. I believe that our spirit guides are with us always, even though we may never learn to hear them or to communicate with them. It helps especially when you feel that there are loving forces around you watching over you and protecting you.

I have been in the fortunate position of having proof of this through the psychic readings I do for people. I have psychically seen many different spirit guides from all cultural backgrounds who are attached to the clients who come to see me for counselling and psychic readings. As I have mentioned elsewhere, our spirit guides are not always known to us, and we can have more than one guide. Each has a special role to play in guiding its subject.

However, making contact with spirit forms through channelling can be quite dangerous if we are not careful in our approach to it. When you open up your mind in channelling, you invite spirits to enter your being. Of course, this is a serious matter as some spirits are good and some are not. If you are sincere, you will largely attract sincere, genuine spirits. However, accidents do happen and a negative or evil spirit may pass through the network of protection given by your spirit guide.

I feel that channelling should be regarded with great respect for the channeller and should not be entered into lightly or out of a sense of disrespect for the whole process. I believe that genuine channellers can receive truth which can often be verified. Sometimes, predictions are made through channelling and sometimes comfort, healing and wisdom are given by this means. But again, you should never attempt this procedure yourself unless you are somewhat spiritually developed and are protected by your guides.

I would now like to share with you some of the teachings of Anna Maree. Our sessions with her were tape recorded and I have taken some of her words to share with you now. The first session is a dialogue between Laurie and Anna Maree about 'planes' and 'levels' of being which will help you to understand the teachings of Anna Maree that follow. Anna Maree spoke of different aspects of life, truth and reality and I have arranged them under the headings: Healing, Faith, Peace and Wisdom.

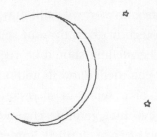

'Planes' and 'levels' of being

Laurie: I'm not clear about planes and levels and so on. You are on the Third Plane. At what level or plane is a human being? Are there human beings on various levels?

Anna Maree: We consider that your plane is separate from our plane. Our planes and spheres come in seven levels. When you pass from an earthly body, you pass into one of the Seven Planes on our sphere, on our side. The plane you choose to enter depends upon your spiritual progress while in an earthly body. For those who are not evolved spiritually, there is the First Plane. On this plane they must acquire all the knowledge that is there for them to absorb before their spiritual progress can take them further. Having absorbed all the knowledge from the First Plane, they are able to travel onwards. Some will go to the Second Plane, others the Third and so on. The final plane is the Seventh Plane. This is the last plane where spiritual beings stay before going eternally to God.

Laurie: The people in an earthly body – can they be existing at, and of, these levels of spiritual development?

Anna Maree: People who exist in an earthly body can evolve, can progress to certain levels – this is true. As you progress in your spiritual growth and in your own awareness levels – in your consciousness – you will attain other levels. This will come through meditation, through reading, through listening to your heart and through finding inner peace. It also comes through giving love to people around you. The more you give, the more you grow. You can have whatever you want, at whatever level you wish, so you may choose to have a physical existence on any one of the planes above.

On our sphere you can choose to wear a physical body or you can choose to have no body. You can have nature around you

– animals, birds, flowers, water, wind, sun, air – if you wish. This is up to you: there is free choice for you to create your own world here. This is a concept which many people do not accept on your sphere. In your physical body you accept what you create for yourself. This same concept follows you when you pass over to our sphere. You choose your own reality!

Laurie: Are we all God returning to ourselves?

Anna Maree: This is indeed true! In the beginning there was only one being, one soul. This was God. He was fragmented, broken up into all the physical manifestations which are now known to you. Each one of you is a spark of God and each one of you will return to God in a perfect state. Your travels through eternity lead to this perfection, and not one of you returns to God without being perfected.

Healing

My name is Anna Maree. I come to you from another world. Tonight we will talk about healing.

Healing is an energy force. It is a combination of what you generate from within the physical body and what we generate from our sphere. When these energies are compatible, healing takes place. Healing comes also when life's problems are eased. We ask that you realise that if everything went smoothly in life you would not grow. In order to grow, you must experience many trials and tribulations. As you accept these, you must also expect change. Accept changes with faith and you will flow with life. Sometimes you will feel disoriented even when you accept these changes. Accept this disorientation and adjust to it, for at the end of it you will see the reason for it. We are always close to you, and simply by thinking about us we are brought closer to you. We detect fear in many earthly beings. If you let go of fear and believe in our protection, there is nothing left to fear.

There is no such thing as a healer. Healing is natural. It comes to you through the elements. The elements are yours. Stop worrying about what you have not, take notice of what you have, and be thankful for it. Appreciate your world, for in your world there is much beauty. This beauty is unseen by so many eyes. Hold no fears, for you have no reason to fear. We are with you. We guide you. We look after you, we keep you near us. Have no fear. Go about your daily lives, happy and content knowing that we are with you. Depression is a thing of the past. Let it go. We want you to be well and whole and happy!

When you believe in our guidance, all the major decisions in your lives will come through your hearts. We communicate with you via your hearts. We ask that you listen to this communication and act on it, for it is our direct telephone line to you. Sometimes it is difficult to know whether the mind or the heart is giving you the answers you seek. Often people know in their hearts what they should do, but their minds tell them something else.

There is a very fine line between the 'mind' and the 'head'. It is not the mind that causes conflict in making the right choices in life. It is in fact the head. The head relates to the physical body. The mind and the head (or the physical) are two different entities altogether, and we believe that so many people are trapped in the physical plane; so many people have their conscious level simply based on the physical. This is why you have people who are murderers, robbers and rapists: they have not yet left their physical being and travelled into their spiritual and their mental being.

We want you to know that natural healing elements are vital in all forms of healing, and wherever possible you should use these natural elements. The natural elements include the sun, wind and rain. There is much healing in the sand and salt water. There is much emotional healing in the breezes. People on your sphere do not know, and are not aware enough of, the natural elements and the healing powers. You should go to the ocean and you should walk with bare feet on the grass. Wherever possible, you should use fresh rainwater for healing, bathing wounds and to take as fluid where necessary. These things have been given to you for a reason.

Colour is a very important part of all healing. It has endless and boundless qualities. For example, when a person is angry, there should not be any red or orange or yellow around them, for these colours stimulate the psychic trigger that starts the action of anger within people. When a psychic person is tuning in to an aura and sees the colour red, it indicates that the person has gone through much anger in recent times or is still experiencing anger.

Blue and green are beautiful, healing colours. When angry, a person should be presented with colours of blue and green, the 'calming' colours. These colours make the soul settle, which helps take away all anger and frustration, and leads the soul into feeling calm and cool.

These are the colours of the sky and the grass, and this is for a very special reason. This is to *anchor* people. When they look up they see the blue of the sky, and when they look down they see the green of the grass under their feet. This anchors them. Between the blue of the sky and the green of the grass lie the souls of people, for the souls of people are in the atmosphere, whether you understand this concept or not.

Every soul that has ever been born on the physical plane remains in the atmosphere between the earth and the sky. This is like the blueprint of the soul, and even when the soul passes on to the spirit world, the blueprint of the soul remains. You experience these blueprints when you encounter ghosts.

You should try to remember how important colour is. Where learning is taking place, the colour yellow should be displayed. This is the colour of intellectualism and we advise that students should utilise the colour yellow.

You can use colour by wearing it or by having it displayed in pictures or in decorations. We also suggest coloured lights. If you need peace and quiet you should have blue light around you.

Music is also a very important part of healing. Any type of music that fits well with the soul is, in fact, healing music. This depends entirely upon the individual. It is up to each one of you to decide on the music that suits your needs. Sometimes lively music is better than slow music. It all depends on how the individual feels at any given time.

If you are feeling lively, then healing can still come

through to you provided you are in tune with the music you are listening to. The same applies to peaceful, reflective music. If you are in a peaceful mood, or wanting to be peaceful, you should listen to quiet, peaceful music. Sometimes it's best not to listen to any music, but rather to tune in to one's own inner music.

With natural healing, there are no barriers. We see the energy forces of the body being reversed where negative forces have taken over. We see these being reversed with positive forces and this, then, is the beginning of true healing. We see medical science becoming more accepting of this natural healing, and we see that over the next fifty years much progress will be made in the field of natural healing.

We ask, then, that the use of colour in healing be recognised, as well as the use of music and sound vibration. We ask also that sunlight and its application to healing be recognised and harnessed. We ask that the elements in sand be recognised as it has many healing components which have not yet been fully understood. We would like to see research taking place in these areas. We see the time when people will not question, but will accept what is so. But such a time is far into your future.

We want you to know that when the body is healed, so is the spirit, and true healing must include body and spirit.

$\mathcal{F}$aith

Each of you is growing from within. We ask that you continue in faith so that your growth may also continue. It is important to recognise that you are growing and that with this growth, of course, comes change. Do not question the change, but rather go with it. It is vitally important that you change, for without change there can be no growth, and without growth your spiritual path does not take you any deeper or any higher.

With change comes the need for more faith. Faith is reuired when your stability is threatened. You must have faith to come through major life crises. It is easy to lose faith; turmoil in your sphere can upset you and throw you off your path, and things do not always go the way you have planned. It is better not to plan too far ahead. Take each day as it comes. We are here to lead you and guide you. We can open doors for you and we ask that you trust and believe. We ask that you listen to your own souls.

Do not hold on to things from the past that no longer fit into your world. Allow these to go, for they no longer serve you. Do not hold regrets, for regrets chain you and keep you down. Let go of all regrets. Let go of all fear, and listen to your heart.

We ask you to keep your faith no matter what comes your way; no matter what obstacles are placed in your path, we ask you to keep your faith. It is easier to throw faith away than to hold on to it. It takes strength and courage to have faith. Only the strong have faith. Be strong and persevere. Faith can move mountains! This is a fact. You can achieve whatever you want when you have enough faith. The stronger the faith, the easier it is to deal with life and all its demands.

We ask that you continue in faith so that your growth may continue also. Have faith and the unknown will become known to you. Do not fear for your future. If you have faith you can create a purposeful future for yourself. Faith will grow the more you experience it. It is everlasting to those who attain it.

$\mathscr{P}$eace

My name is Anna Maree. I come to you from another world. Tonight we will talk about peace.

Peace comes with knowledge and knowledge comes with wisdom. Wisdom is the all-powerful and almighty truth, unadulterated, unchanged, given to you (on earth) as it comes direct from our sphere. Peace comes after you have absorbed this knowledge, this wisdom, this truth, directly into your heart. Peace comes with knowing that we in our sphere care for you from our plane and look after you. We guide you and keep you and we are with you eternally.

Peace is the knowledge that comes with letting go. Let go of your fears, hopes and plans and be guided by what comes to you. We know what is right for you; we look after you and we keep you. When you can do this, when you give yourselves over to us, you will find this inner peace which everyone searches for and which so few people find. Peace comes to you to protect you, to keep you from harm, and to be with you always.

When you attain this peace, you will find that it comes to you from the very depths of your being, from the very depths of your soul. You will find when you attain peace, that your total being comes into alignment; your physical, emotional, mental and spiritual beings all come into alignment and you will feel a glowing feeling from within. This peace can be yours for all time. This peace can stay with you throughout your entire existence.

Whatever is happening in your life, whatever trouble you are going through, whatever darkness you are experiencing, you can still find this peace if you give yourself what we allow you to have: this trust in the feeling that we are with you all the time, and we *are* with you. We are here to guide you. We are here to look after you and to take you along dark and narrow paths. We ask that you trust us and come to us in faith, for we will lead you along the right paths. Sometimes, these are dark and deep, but if you have faith you will find that the peace within you will help you through.

So many people on your plane strive for peace and yet they are looking in the wrong places. They expect to find peace through gaining material things, through being on top in whatever they are doing. Material existence does not necessarily lead to peace. Peace comes from deep within your own being. Peace comes with knowledge and trust. Peace comes after you let go of fear.

As your guides, we will lead you along the right paths. We will enfold you and keep you with us. Please understand that even the dark, sometimes very narrow paths are necessary for you to travel along so that you will grow. It is necessary for you to understand that life for you is a period of growth and of the attainment of goals, which you choose before you enter your earthly body. You can attain these goals in peaceful fashion, even though you may suffer. It is possible to suffer and yet be at peace. All suffering leads to growth and all growth leads to peace. For no matter what doors close in your lives, there will be more doors open to you and these doors will lead you along better and brighter paths.

If human beings could learn to listen to the peace within their own hearts, to tune in to their guides, to listen to their own being, then there would be no wars. We see from our sphere much trouble on your sphere. We see the word peace being bandied around without any meaning. We see the futility of the talks amongst the major powers about peace. We see the war growing and we see many people dying and we feel sorry that so many people are caught up in useless wars. The word peace at this time is so vitally important for it is a time when human beings must find peace within their own souls.

Where true peace is found, there is no illness in the physical body. True peace brings total unity to all beings. People hold on to illness because they are not at peace. People seek illness, for they are searching for something they cannot name. They are hiding, running away; they are not at peace.

Many people suffer needlessly, for the truth has not yet been revealed to them. If people would listen to their hearts and have faith and learn to love themselves then they will find true harmony and peace, as peace and growth become one. With one comes the other.

Inner peace comes after periods of struggle. Some people enter their physical bodies in peaceful fashion and maintain a peaceful life. They leave the physical body in the same peaceful fashion. Quite often these people are highly developed souls. People who are able to cope well with life's problems are often people who have travelled many times in physical bodies. They have reincarnated often.

When you are at your lowest point, please remember that we are with you. We ask you to feel the depths of your being, feel right into your heart, into your soul, and as you reach into your own being you will find us there. You will find peace, for each one of you has the capacity to find peace and contentment. You must allow yourself to let go of fear – to let go of being afraid of the unknown – for all is well. Have faith and the unknown will become known to you. Do not fear for the future – you are not alone.

Wisdom

What is wisdom? Wisdom is the knowledge that we gain from truth. Wisdom comes only in pure form. Many people are confused about what truth is. Many people absorb untruths and believe these to be true. Wisdom is in itself pure truth. It is difficult for people on your sphere to discern what is in fact truth and what is not truth. Many people realise that if they are told something often enough, they will absorb it and take it as truth. This, over the years, becomes false wisdom based on a false premise. False wisdom is very deceptive, for it clouds and colours people's beliefs and ideas and can cause much suffering.

In accepting wisdom, you must always decipher it for yourselves. Simply because something has been told to you, or because you have read it and absorbed it does not mean it is wisdom, it does not mean it is truth. Many people in the scientific field believe that they have found wisdom. However, there is a higher truth that also operates and the two factions should meet. Science alone is not enough. The only way you can distinguish real truth from untruth is by listening to your own heart. For within your heart is true wisdom.

Wisdom is pure thought and it comes in the pure thought form. Human beings have the capacity to tap into this pure thought form and to absorb wisdom for themselves. You can build up your own collection of wisdom by tapping into this source. From this same source come healing energies, for healing energy and wisdom are in fact the same force.

For anything to work completely it must be in pure form. Wisdom is, in fact, pure form when it comes to you through listening to your heart. This is so for healing as well. It comes to you in pure form. Anything tainted is not pure form and therefore not the real thing. You must learn to distinguish between what is real and what is human interpretation. Wisdom is knowledge gained over the centuries. All knowledge and all thought forms remain in the atmosphere.

Knowledge is as 'real' as love, beauty and electricity. Knowledge is as 'real' as growth. Wisdom is a form of knowledge that has been accumulated over time. We in our sphere have what are known as 'Halls of Learning'. In these Halls of Learning, we store wisdom; we store pure knowledge. From this pure knowledge, human beings absorb ideas on your plane. We 'broadcast' to you and from this broadcast we send knowledge from our sphere to yours.

What you would see as an 'invention' or a new idea is simply knowledge that is picked up by a person who is open to receiving knowledge from our sphere. When this person obtains the knowledge it is in pure form. It is what happens *after* the brain has received this knowledge that can cause problems. If people would take this knowledge in pure form and leave it at that – without changing it and adding their own interpretations to it – then it would, in fact, be wisdom. Unfortunately, this does not always happen and so when people first get ideas for new inventions they misinterpret pure thought form by adding their own ideas. The pure thought form is then tainted and does not work. It often takes many years to perfect the original idea.

People should learn to use this knowledge without adding their own interpretations to it. What they should do is obtain this knowledge and then put it into their heart and absorb it in pure form. At this time, there is so much impure knowledge in this collection of ideas of wisdom that it is very difficult for anyone to obtain pure wisdom on your sphere. This is why you have difficulties; why people can become so confused about what is real and what is not – what is illusion and what is reality.

Reality is an illusion!

If people could learn to leave themselves out and absorb what is there for them in the atmosphere in the way of pure wisdom, then they would advance much faster than they now do. It is simple. When interpreting knowledge and wisdom, you should allow your mind to be totally free. To obtain the knowledge that comes in the broadcast from our sphere to yours, you should allow your own mind to be totally void. Allow your mind to be empty and in so doing you can tap into this knowledge which comes from our sphere. We are constantly broadcasting on our sphere from our Halls of Learning.

People will interpret truth in their own way. Given in pure thought form, our truth is accurate. However, it may be altered by people. If you could learn to tune in to this by listening to your heart, you would know what is truth, what is wisdom and what is tainted knowledge.

All wisdom and real truth are stored. This is why our Halls of Learning are so large. Every thought form remains in the atmosphere and is preserved. In our Halls of Learning we store only pure thought forms. Any other thought form, which is not pure, is allowed to remain in the atmosphere and this is where people often tap in and pick up wrong information.

It is rare to find a soul who is perfectly capable of interpreting pure thought form. There are some people on your sphere who have the capacity to pick up pure thought form. This is because they have the ability to clear their minds to a great extent. We also want you to know that even wisdom in its highest form will remain always basically the same but human beings have free will and can therefore interpret this to their own ends.

Human beings can change the path upon which they travel. Free will is a gift given to all by God. Free will is not interfered with by those on our sphere. Free will is necessary for the progression of humanity.

You should clear your mind of knowledge and wisdom that are not true. You should clear out your mind and eliminate any such knowledge. You should do this consciously, for in clearing the space you allow your higher mind to take over.

There was much wisdom in the ancient religions. Many of the ancient writings are in fact truth. We see that people who follow the religion of Buddhism have found much wisdom. Many of the teachings of Buddha are viable and true. Buddha received his wisdom in pure thought. Buddha did not taint his wisdom with his own mind; he received his knowledge and allowed it to come through in pure thought form. Unfortunately, over the years people have added to these teachings, but the original concepts are pure. People would do well to study the religion of Buddha.

We speak now of the wisdom gained through meditation. When people meditate they travel through their own mind and receive the knowledge from our Halls of Learning. Through our direct broadcast, they can tune in and pick up pure wisdom. People must learn to accept this pure wisdom without adding their own interpretation. Any knowledge that comes through meditation is pure thought form. If you practise meditation every day you will find that you will become clearer and more able to absorb wisdom and truth to assist you in your life.

If you would like to become a wiser person, then tune in to your own self more. Learn to 'read' yourself by meditating and following your heart more. You will have a more fulfilling existence and experience more peace and joy.

Part four

Case studies

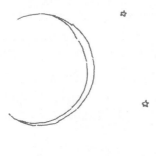

My work as a psychic reader is both exhilarating and rewarding, as you will see in the following case studies, and indeed as you have seen in my story so far. But sometimes I am unable to make a great difference in people's lives, as destiny is such a great force that it can not be interfered with. One client who taught me this valuable lesson was a woman called Suzanna.

When clients arrive at my home, I usually usher them into my office where I seat them in a comfortable chair opposite me. This I did with Suzanna. As she sat down I could see that she was quite ill. She asked me to tune in to her. I saw that Suzanna was terminally ill with cancer, and that she had come to terms with her illness and the fact that she would soon die.

It was difficult to relay this to her, but I had to deliver the information about her health as I received it. She was very accepting of all that I told her about her health, and about her past and present. She reassured me that she did not expect a miracle and we became good friends. I saw Suzanna a few more times and we became closer as her health began to deteriorate further. Eventually she told me that she wanted her life to end as the pain had become too much to bear. As I hugged her goodbye I knew that I would not see her again.

Suzanna died shortly afterwards, and her ashes were scattered in the lovely garden of her beach-side home ...

I am now going to share with you some of the stories I have chosen from amongst the many fascinating case studies I have gathered over the years. Thankfully they have happier endings.

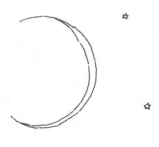

Michelle

One evening, a friend asked me to give him some psychic assistance. He is a general practitioner. As such, he sees many hundreds of patients and generally they respond to their medical treatments. However, he had been having some problems with a particular patient who did not respond to conventional treatment.

He asked me if I would tune in to his patient to see if I could assist. I needed to know the patient's name and age. He gave me this information. In fact, the patient was a baby of eighteen months and her name was Michelle. I remember also asking for the mother's first name and being told it was Jan.

I tuned in. I was of the immediate impression that the baby had been covered with spots of some kind. This was confirmed by my doctor friend. He told me that the baby had broken out in lumps and had a very severe case of diarrhoea. She had been suffering for more than a week and was not responding to the antihistamine injections he had been administering.

I told my friend to tell the mother, Jan, that her daughter should not be given any more stewed apple. I also recommended that the baby should no longer be sleeping under the orange-coloured rug which I could see in my mind's eye. My friend listened to the information and told me he would let me know the outcome.

A week later he telephoned. A very excited voice on the telephone line hastened to tell me how 'amazed and excited' he was with what had occurred. He spoke to Jan, bravely, and asked her about the orange-coloured rug that the baby slept under. She said that it was a synthetic sleeping bag. My friend explained that the lumps were being caused by an allergy to the synthetic cloth of the bag, relaying the information I had given him psychically. The mother was stunned to hear that the doctor even knew the colour of the rug, so when he went on to ask her why she was feeding the baby stewed apple, she was even more stunned. She wanted to know how he knew this information because she had never mentioned it to him.

'I have a psychic friend,' he told her. She listened intently when he told her not to feed the baby any more stewed apple, as it was making the diarrhoea worse.

One week after stopping the stewed apple and placing the baby under cotton and woollen bed linen, the lumps and diarrhoea cleared up completely. My doctor friend was thrilled with the results he was able to achieve with a little psychic help.

John

My friend John, the television director I have mentioned earlier in this book, has also had some interesting psychic sessions with me. One session we both remember well is one we had before he was to film a live spectacular show.

John had a tight schedule, so he wanted to know if I could 'see' any problems with the shoot. I tuned in and told him to expect some problems with a helicopter he was planning to use for some aerial shots. I also saw one of the dancers damaging a muscle in her leg and a tree falling down and causing a few problems. I also saw a blue-coloured light toppling over. I usually do not see negative events, but somehow on this day I did see these unfortunate events taking place. As it happened, the problems I foresaw all occurred ...

The problem with the helicopter was a major one as far as the filming of the show was concerned. It arrived an hour late and the pilot had removed a door for the aerial filming. Unfortunately, it was on the wrong side of the helicopter, so the planned shots could not be taken. The helicopter was having problems with takeoff and, in the end, the whole idea of using it for filming had to be abandoned. Later that morning, it was revealed that the main gyro had malfunctioned. John had told only one person – the production manager – about my predictions concerning the problems with the helicopter.

John set up an alternative camera angle to film from the ground. As the music blared across the small harbour, one of the female dancers fell down in excruciating pain. She had pulled the hamstring in her right leg!

That afternoon, during a break in filming, the crew was all seated around a picnic bench in a nearby park. Suddenly, a loud crackling sound was heard, and the company dived for cover. A large branch of a gum tree above the bench came crashing down on top of the bench and the seats around it. Luckily, no-one was injured – they were just a little shaken! At this point, John told the crew of the session he had had with me and revealed to them the predictions I had made. 'Well, we won't have to worry about a blue light falling,' someone commented, 'because we're not using any blue lights.' The rest of the production went without a hitch.

About a week later, John was again filming, this time a television variety show. The 'live' audience gave an enthusiastic ovation to the taped dance number, which was part of the show. John had been quite concerned about the possibility of a blue light falling (as I had predicted) so he made sure that none of the stage lights

had any blue gels in them. Green, purple, pink – yes. But definitely no blue!

As the two-hour-long show neared its conclusion, John remarked from his control room how lucky it was that none of the lights had fallen. But just as the host of the show was singing the closing number, there was an almighty crashing sound. The people in the audience dived for cover to a chorus of loud screams. A blue light had broken away from the ceiling and had crashed down into the audience, hitting one man heavily on the head.

All four predictions had finally materialised.

$\mathcal{B}$ill

I find that being psychic can be entertaining at times when life could otherwise be a little boring. I remember an example of this when I was living in the country recently.

My husband Bruce and I had moved to a new area and were operating a general medical practice. I was working as a secretary and Bruce was working as a general practitioner in his own practice. We were obliged to attend various medical dinners which were organised from time to time by medical representatives from drug companies. I often found these evenings somewhat draining, as drugs, disease and statistics are not my favourite topics for discussion.

One Friday evening, we arrived at a luxury resort for yet another sales dinner. I decided to make the most of this particular evening, and found myself seated opposite a young male sales rep named Bill, whom I had never met before. He seemed very interested in his work as he chatted away, telling us about his life – past and present – which appeared to be full of excitement and adventure. He told us of his life overseas, where he worked as a ski instructor and tennis coach to some of the world's most interesting people.

Some people have the knack of making life sound wonderful, as though every second of their life is filled with great adventure. Bill certainly had this talent. However, I wondered to myself what he was really like beneath the bubble and froth on the surface. As he babbled on, I tuned in to him. I normally do not do this, as I don't like to invade people's privacy, but on this night I was feeling decidedly defiant and bored!

I began to concentrate on his energy. I picked up that Bill was, in fact, quite lonely. I could see that he lived alone and was pining after a lost love. I felt that a blonde woman was quite close to him, but that she lived interstate. He was missing her. I also felt that she was questioning the relationship, as she had another love as well. Bill would need to woo her more solidly if he was hoping to 'win' her. I kept this information to myself and pondered about it as Bruce and I drove along a country road later that evening.

As we were nearing the turn-off to our home, Bruce asked me how I had enjoyed the evening. I chatted on about my thoughts and then I mentioned that I felt that Bill was entertaining and also quite unhappy. Bruce found this hard to believe, as it appeared that Bill was on top of the world. I told Bruce what I had seen psychically about Bill. He listened but didn't comment.

A couple of weeks later, Bill walked into the surgery. I greeted him and ushered him into the consulting room, where Bruce had a few spare minutes between patients. Bill and he began to chat, so I shut the door and left them to it.

Some time later, Bill left the room and walked towards me with a big smile. He gave me a hug. I was quite surprised, because I didn't feel that I had earned this show of affection. He winked at me and said he'd see us that night. He had invited us to dinner at the motel where he was staying.

Bill greeted us warmly that evening and we settled in to enjoy fine food and his good company. It became clear that he wanted to chat about how I possibly could have known all the things Bruce had relayed to him about what I had 'seen' in his life. (And I thought *women* gossiped!) It was clear that what I had felt – about the girlfriend interstate and his unhappy heart – was correct and Bill wanted some answers! We had a very interesting discussion that night.

For me, there was a bonus. It turned out that Bill was the brother of a friend of mine, Jill, whom I had not seen for eighteen years! We had begun our teaching careers together and had become firm friends. Jill and I had lost contact over the years, but I had thought about her often. Bill gave me her current address and telephone number. I looked forward to catching up with my long-lost friend.

What a funny world!

$\mathcal{D}$ ieter

Some of my most interesting cases have involved health issues. One of the most memorable involved a young man named Dieter. Dieter had heard about the work we were doing through a friend of his who had been to visit.

When he was fifteen years old, Dieter had suffered a most unfortunate accident. During an experiment in a science laboratory at school, a beaker had shattered while being heated by a Bunsen burner and he had been cut by flying glass. As a result, he had developed a rather severe ulcer on the leg below his knee. The ulcer refused to heal and no amount of medical treatment and care was bringing results. When Dieter visited John and me, he was despondent because the doctor had booked him into hospital to have his leg amputated below the knee.

I felt his despair as I tuned in to him. I concentrated hard and John wrote the treatments down as I reeled them off. Dieter would need to follow a very strict regimen of diet, herbs and vitamins. After this advice was delivered, John and I turned our attention to psychic healing. We poured energy into the patient. It was hard for Dieter to comprehend what was taking place, but he was desperate to save his leg and any help was worth a try. He left two hours later, promising to let us know what happened at the hospital a week later.

The next week, I received a huge bunch of flowers; what a gorgeous display! With them was a note that read: 'Ulcer healing well! Love, Dieter.' He phoned us a few days later from his home. He told me that as he was being examined at the hospital just before his operation, the doctor was quite amazed to find a pulse in his leg below the knee. This meant, of course, that the blood was now flowing to the affected area. The ulcer was beginning to heal. The operation was cancelled and Dieter was sent home to continue his healing process.

I offered a prayer of thanks to the powers that be!

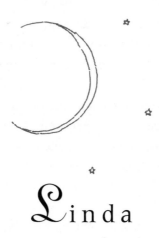

$\mathcal{L}$inda

Linda was a bright and happy woman in her early twenties. She came in for a psychic reading one morning and I found it easy to tune in to her. As the session proceeded, I could see that there was to be a wedding for her quite soon. She beamed and agreed that this was correct. I tuned in and saw a dark-haired man, who I knew would make a wonderful husband. I told her he was thirty-three years old. When I announced this, Linda's smile disappeared and she exclaimed that I had made a mistake. Her husband-to-be was fair, and twenty-seven years old. I had the wrong man.

I concentrated even more deeply. No, I could not see a fair man. I *could* see only a dark thirty-three-year-old man. I insisted that Linda would marry the dark man.

A few weeks later, I heard that Linda had married a fair man, aged twenty-seven. 'Oh, dear,' I thought. 'I was picking up the wrong information – but it had been so clear!' I didn't understand what had gone wrong. I decided to get on with things and not let this throw me off my work. I continued to do readings and I became busier and busier.

Two or three months later, Linda booked in for another reading. She was quite distressed. I took her into the room and sat her in a comfortable armchair. She insisted that I tune in and tell her what I now saw. Again, I saw the dark-haired, thirty-three-year-old man. I told her that they would wed.

She broke down and sobbed. She explained that her recent marriage to the fair-haired man had been a most unhappy mistake. She had, in fact, met a dark-haired, thirty-three-year-old man with whom she had fallen madly in love. He felt the same. This was an awkward situation as she was now married. She had decided to seek a divorce, even though she'd been married only three and a half months. Her husband happily consented to the divorce as he, too, was unhappy.

Now, many years later, Linda is very happily married to the dark-haired man and they are the proud parents of two beautiful, dark-haired boys!

Life is strange sometimes!

Conclusion

Looking forward, looking back

*T*hroughout this book I have recounted some of the experiences in my life that have contributed to or affected my psychic development.

In my work with people I am constantly learning. My clients teach me new things every day. Their guides teach me new things every day. It is a privilege to be alive to experience the happiness and the difficult times that we each encounter on our journey through life.

It has been rewarding, exciting, exhilarating and wonderful, but it has not been easy. It has never been easy. To a great extent I have had to sacrifice my own will for the sake of my growth and development. Often this has led to pain and a great deal of sadness and suffering for myself, and even worse, for my family who I love.

When my psychic and spiritual awareness began to develop, I consciously needed to weigh up my actions and the effect they would have on myself and those around me. There is truly 'no gain without pain'. It would be wonderful to grow without causing harm to others, but realistically I don't believe this can be achieved. If you are brave enough to choose to grow in spiritual awareness then you will need to make difficult choices in your life. Provided your motivations are pure, and your aim is to give back to life what you learn so that others will ultimately benefit, then you will succeed in your quest for truth.

Learning about the spiritual realm, where reality is so vastly different from the 'reality' of life on earth, is confronting, and old belief systems are up for scrutiny. You will begin to see the world through very different eyes. If you succeed in your quest, always questioning your own integrity and motivation, you will eventually reach a state of unconditional love. Here you will see life – every aspect of it – in a new way. You will begin to feel bonded to all of creation and all its colours, sounds, tastes and feelings. You will begin to admire people of all colours, all religions, all ages and from all walks of life. There is beauty in everyone. This is the key to discovering the secrets of life. It will become easy to know things about people; to see their past, their present and their future. It starts with love and a sense of oneness with all souls.

Psychic awareness is available to anyone who seeks it. You do not have to be special or different to access this knowledge. All you need is a genuine desire to use the information in a safe and useful way to be of benefit to yourself and to others. You will need to be courageous and thick-skinned. Many will criticise you and misinterpret you along the way. You will appear selfish and you will need to live your life as an example to others. It is not easy. Retreat will constantly beckon you, and you will often think it's easier to be caught in a world of darkness. But do persist.

It is truly worthwhile.

If you would like to contact the author, write to

Beverley Litchfield
PO Box 176
Beecroft NSW 2119

EMBRACED
BY THE
LIGHT
BETTY J. EADIE

Betty Eadie 'died' after an operation, but was later to recover. It was during the intervening period of a few hours that she had what has been described as 'the most profound near-death experience ever'. Her description of her experience in this astonishing book is one of the most convincing arguments for the existence of life after death.

There is a great secret contained in Embraced by the Light. *It is something that the great prophets and spiritual leaders have tried to tell us for thousands of years. Betty Eadie learned it by nearly dying. It has the power to change your life.*

Melvin Morse M. D.
Best-selling author of
Transformed by the Light and
Closer to the Light

ISBN 1855 385 104

Aquarian/Thorsons
An Imprint of HarperCollinsPublishers

BEYOND
THE
LIGHT
P. M. H. ATWATER

P. M. H. Atwater 'died' three times in 1977. Since then she has devoted her life to understanding the near-death experience, and has spoken to thousands of survivors. What she has learned will startle you, perhaps disturb you, and just might change your life.

This is an in-depth, comprehensive look at the near-death phenomenon and its after-effects and implications. Atwater challenges the stereotype of the tunnel of light, and presents provocative evidence of many different types of experience, including the hell-like as well as the transcendent. She also describes the experiences of people who were dead for several days and then revived, and of those who attempted suicide.

ISBN 1855 384 248

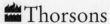Thorsons
An Imprint of HarperCollins*Publishers*